# Get Up, Get Out, & Get Something

## How Contrapreneurship Can Help You Build a Booming Business

*The Ruckers,*
*Blessings!*

## JEROME LOVE

J LOVELY PUBLISHING

# Get Up, Get Out, & Get Something

## How Contrapreneurship Can Help You Build a Booming Business

Jerome Love, J Lovely Publishing

Published by J Lovely Publishing

P.O. Box 710474 Houston, TX 77071

Tel (888) 225-1918

info@jeromelove.com

www.jeromelove.com

Cover Design: Majestic Design Group, www.MajesticDesignGroup.com

Photography by: Grady Carter & Just In Time Photography, www.jitphotography.com

# CONTENTS

# INTRODUCTION

One of the people who encouraged me to write this book was my good friend, college classmate and fellow contrapreneur, Jonathan Sprinkles. When we began, he asked me a simple question: "Who's your book for?" I thought for a minute, and then I responded. "This book is for me in 1998 when I started my first business."

Like many, I had a desire to break away from corporate America, but this idea was contra to everything I'd been taught. I was raised to believe you get a good education and you'll get a good job. It wasn't long before I began to see that wasn't totally true.

I now realize that there are millions of people out there who are going through some of the same things I was experiencing in 1998. I dedicate this book to all of you. If you're wondering whether you have what it takes to start and run a successful business - you do. If you've already launched your business, and you're wondering if you made the right decision - you did.

It is my firm belief that the only way to ensure your personal and financial freedom is by pursuing your entrepreneurial ambitions. I also am convinced that there is really no such thing as a "good job." Leaving corporate America was the best decision I could have ever made.

You don't have to be a business owner to appreciate the lessons in Contrapreneurship. If success from the inside out is what you seek — read this book. It's filled with strategies that will challenge you to play the game of life and business at a whole new level.

My journey has been an interesting one — full of blessings and hard-knock lessons — but I have to say that I've learned so much about myself, about life and of course, about business over the past several years. By embarking on your own contrapreneurial adventure, you too will experience a whole new world of possibilities.

Here's to your unimaginable success!

Jerome Love

**www.jeromelove.com**

# ONE

# What Is Contrapreneurship?

---

"The Houston Black Expo has become the "must attend" business expo in Texas because of Jerome's vision, determination and most importantly, his contrapreneurial spirit."

*—Fran Harris, Ph.D., National Television Personality, Inspirational*

*Speaker and Author of Will The Real You Please Stand Up? 7*

*Strategies To Help You Discover Your Purpose & Live It With Passion*

Every world-class athlete knows one thing: in order to become faster, better and physically stronger, he or she must incorporate some kind of "resistance" work into their training regime. Like our modern-day athletic counterparts, champion-level business owners know that to succeed in business, we, too must be willing to resist the status quo. We must be willing to tax our intellectual limits and known financial boundaries. We must be willing to look risk square in the face and do the thing that no one else dares to do. We must be a Contrapreneur - a person who goes against type, tradition, convention and yes, sometimes common sense. Of course, the thing that's most interesting about common sense is that it's not as common as most of us think it is!

Our country's greatest innovations are the result of the ingenuity of individuals whose thoughts and actions were "contra" to tradition or "contra" to convention. Agricultural chemist George Washington Carver refused a $100,000 a year salary so that he could study peanuts. Although he did study other

> A Contrapreneur is a person who goes against type, tradition, convention and yes, sometimes common sense. But perhaps the most distinguishing trait of all contrapreneurs is the desire to drastically transform the way we live our everyday lives or do business.

things, he was essentially a peanut farmer. His refusal of income that was equivalent to about a million dollars today had everyone around him baffled, but he didn't let tradition stifle his creativity.

George Washington Carver was a Contrapreneur. He consciously went against the norm and stayed true to his own pursuits. He also discovered over 300 uses for the peanut. That's contrapreneurship in living color.

Media mogul Oprah Winfrey was told to straighten her hair, get a nose job and go to charm school if she had any aspirations of being a serious on-air television personality. Instead of enrolling in charm school, she went against the established look and sound of network television, built an enviable media empire and became the country's first self-made African-American female billionaire. That's contrapreneurship in action.

Bill Gates developed a fascination with computers at an early age. Like most children of the '60s, he was told that the key to success was going to college and getting a good job. He enrolled in Harvard University but never lost his enchantment with computers. A few years after enrolling, he dropped out of Harvard, followed his own intuition and built, arguably one of the most innovative personal computing and software companies our country will ever know. His family wealth is reported to be second only to the Walton family. That's contrapreneurship on steroids.

What's most fascinating about these mega-success stories is that these individuals weren't born with platinum spoons in their mouths. They weren't given superpowers at birth. They were ordinary humans with extraordinary drive and determination. But perhaps the most distinguishing trait of all contrapreneurs is the desire to drastically transform the way we live our everyday lives or do business. Carver's persistence with peanuts led to additional innovations in agriculture. Winfrey's shattering of the glass TV lens changed the complexion of daytime television. And Bill Gates single handedly revolutionized the personal computer business.

One thing that I've found to be true is that the vast majority of the population has some type of entrepreneurial ambitions. I believe we were born to be innovators and creators. It's who we are. However, the American educational system is designed to take away that sense of creativity, instead opting to teach us to stay within the lines and not to think outside of the box. As a result, most of the people working regular nine to fives are not satisfied with their lives, because they're not doing what they were created to do. These people are unhappy with what they have in life and they are also afraid to step out and try something different. In many ways, I understand, because this is how I felt during my brief stint in corporate America. We'll get to that in a minute. For now, know one important truth: you were born to be great. You were also born to do great things.

My sincere desire is to follow in the footsteps of contrapreneurs like Gates, Winfrey and Carver and others whose contributions continue to change the world. Each day I'm faced with amazing challenges, but contrapreneurship gives me the chance to leave an indelible mark on the world through my business, service and philanthropic efforts. And despite what you may have been taught all your life, contrapreneurship will lead you closer to your entrepreneurial dreams and ideally, financial freedom, causing you to never look at business the same.

Guaranteed!

# TWO

# A Contrapreneur In Progress

---

"Contrapreneurship is a must for anyone who wants to know the real deal about starting a business. Jerome is a true business leader and at age 30 he has achieved more than most strive for in a lifetime."

**—Dana Carson, M.Div. Ph.D., Founder and Senior Pastor,**

**The Reflections of Christ's Kingdom World Outreach Intl.**

**CEO, Dana Carson Ministries, Inc.**

Get Up, Get Out, Get Something. It's more than just the title of this book. It was actually the name of my first business. I was a junior in college at The University of Texas at Austin. It was a time when the urban clothing market was really starting to take off. My idea was to launch a motivational line of clothing called GUGOGS, which stands of course, for Get Up, Get Out, Get Something. I was full of unstoppable youth and optimism, and believed that anything was possible. I was my own boss, and was fascinated by the fact that I was no longer dependent upon someone else to write me a check. I wrote my own checks!

Although I firmly believe that having a business is the best way to make a living, the reality is that it was not my original intention to start my own business. It was a journey that started with a simple college internship.

During my sophomore and junior years in college, I did two internships in corporate America. Each of those internships was at a major car rental company. My official title was Management Trainee, and my job entailed a wide array of duties from prepping cars, picking up customers, writing contracts, and even selling insurance. I was the one who convinced you to buy a $30 damage waiver on a $20-a-day car. It was a very fast-paced job that was fun at the beginning, but later grew to be boring and monotonous.

My first day on the job was nothing special. I wore the standard company clothing: a white or blue dress shirt with a solid colored tie to match, and a pair of business slacks. My first day consisted of many of the duties of car prep, namely washing cars in the hot Texas sun, which meant that by the end of my shift I was drenched. Occasionally, the manager allowed me to pick a customer up or drop one off. Although washing cars all day wasn't exactly my idea of working in corporate America, I remained upbeat and happy. The highlight of my day was when we got a call from another branch in need of one of our luxury cars.

The company that I worked for had several locations in the Austin area, and it was common to swap cars. My task was to take a brand new emerald green Cadillac from the north side of town to the south side, about a 30-minute drive. At first, I was shocked that they'd trust me with this brand new luxury car, but the idea grew on me, and the next thing I knew I was on my way. Before leaving, I made sure to get a few tapes from my personal car to properly test the sound system in the Caddy. Needless to say it was a great ride dropping off the car. I drove as slowly as possible to make sure everyone could see me. It was great! Within a day or two of the drop-off, I began writing contracts and engaging in customer sales.

As a 19-year-old intern, I led my branch — and the area — in sales. In the sales department, there were two key categories: upgrades and damage waiver sales. Upgrades were just as they sounded: upgrading people from one class of car to another. For instance, if a person asked for a compact car for $29.99 a day, my goal was to get them into a full size or luxury vehicle, ranging anywhere from $59.99 a day to $89.99 a day. Hey, don't get mad at me, I was just doing my job!

Damage waiver sales were essentially selling insurance to the customers on the cars. Both of these areas were exceptionally challenging, as our branch was one that primarily serviced a few major dealerships and body shops. Thus, the vast majority of the people that came through our doors weren't in the best of moods to begin with. They'd either had a car that had broken down on them and was now in the shop, or they'd been involved in a car accident. Some were fighting with insurance companies and I'd estimate that more than 90 percent of them were spending money on unplanned repairs. Therefore, their mindset was to spend as little money as possible.

Customers came in all shapes, sizes and colors, each with

different backgrounds and economic profiles that I was able to sum up in one of three categories. The most common customer was what I called the Persistent Pessimist. These were the ones

> I was making this company tens of thousands of dollars on a monthly basis yet my bank account wasn't reflecting the financial gains. What was worse than not being paid well was that I had no life outside of the job.

who were mad at life and the world. These people felt that everyone was out to get them, and life wasn't fair. The Pessimist was difficult, but not as difficult as the next type, Mr. Know It All. These people tended to be a bit more relaxed and calm. Most were white-collar professionals that always wanted to be in control. They weren't that emotional. Plus, they had a plan for everything. When you offered them the insurance, they'd immediately begin explaining all of the intricate details of their current policy. Then of course, they'd explain that even if their current policy didn't cover them, surely their platinum credit card would.

Lastly, you had my favorite type of customer, the Eternal

Optimist. These were the people that came in laughing and joking. No matter how negative the situation, they were optimistic that it would work out. The optimists were always a lot of fun, and it was easy to build a rapport with them.

The typical process of making a sale would go as follows; We would get a call from a dealership or body shop, and my manager would send me to do a pick-up. I would always pick the biggest and prettiest luxury car, drive to the dealership, find the customer, and then direct them to the shiny new car. My immediate goal was to establish some type of relationship or rapport with them by making small talk. All of this was designed to calm the person and take their mind off of their car. As the customers talked, I listened carefully to what they had to say. I realized the importance of being able to connect with them so that I could figure out the best way to meet their needs. Once we got back to the office, I would get them coffee or water as we continued the conversation. Now, some people would call this level of salesmanship "sucking up." I call it carving out the path to becoming the number 1 salesperson on the team and in the area!

After the customer settled in, we would move on to filling out the paperwork. I found that most people don't like filling out paperwork or contracts, so I'd do my best to make them feel as though they were NOT doing paperwork. I had my system down-pat, and as a result, I was the top salesman in the company and was recognized monthly as one of the rising stars. In addition to my whopping $7 an hour salary, I was regularly invited to dinners or lunches at fancy restaurants with a lot of the corporate big wigs.

At first, it was fun and exciting to have dinner with the branch and regional managers at some of Austin's elite eateries. All of my peers sang my praises and looked up to me. Yet, beyond the steak dinners and all of the accolades, I began to feel somewhat unappreciated, overworked and underpaid. I was making this company tens of thousands of dollars on a monthly basis, yet my bank account wasn't reflecting the financial gains. What was worse than not being paid well was that I had no life outside of the job.

- 6:00 a.m. wake up
- 6:45 a.m. leave for work
- 7:15 a.m. get to work

- 7:30 a.m.   to 6:00 p.m. work
- 6:45 p.m.   get home
- 7:30 p.m.   eat dinner
- 9:00 p.m.   watch Seinfeld reruns
- 10:00 p.m.  go to be bed

Each day the tedious cycle began all over again. Instead of being a corporate hot shot, I was more like a paid robot. I no longer had time to hang out with my friends, nor go to the gym as regularly anymore. It was a horrible feeling, and I couldn't see myself doing this for the rest of my life. Something had to change.

> I was being hindered because I was doing as I was told
> and working my life away at my "good job".

I was 19 years old, working, on average, 60 hours weekly, which equaled only $420 a week! Here I was, busting my butt to increase my sales in order to make this company more money, and all I got in return was $420 a week? My life was worth only

$420 a week? To me it didn't add up, and I knew there had to be a better way.

I soon began to think about my future with the company as they were trying to prepare me, their little superstar, for management. But what was there to look forward to? Larger checks? More steak dinners?

At the time, branch managers made a base of roughly $65,000 annually, plus commissions on their branch. Area managers made a base of $110,000, plus commissions on all the branches in their region. Couple that with the fact that the typical track to management took about two years. To the average Joe, this scenario might have appeared somewhat appealing. It was tempting, trust me. But something deep down within me would not allow me to accept the fact that my life was only worth $110,000.

Six figures, while enticing, seemed like so little, even to a guy who was making only $420 a week. Still I was intrigued. So, I began to delve more into the lives of management. Managers were the first to arrive and the last to leave. They were there on weekends. They had to make all of the after-hour mixers to hob knob with the other corporate folks, which was critical to their progression in the company. The job was their whole world, and their identity was wrapped up in their title or job. I realized that they were trading their lives for a career with a company that lured them with the empty promise of making more money. It just didn't add up.

Shortly thereafter, I made the decision not to exchange my life for $110,000 a year. I knew I was worth more than that. In addition, I realized that it was really pointless to have a big house if I lived alone or was never there because I worked too much. Just as having a big bank account is pointless if you have no time to enjoy your money. Many people can't see or don't realize this, because society has conditioned us to think that "outside" success is the ultimate prize. Get an education, so you can get a "good job." Ever heard that before? The contrapreneur inside of me (that I didn't even know was there) didn't allow me to settle for this. As a result, I began a quest for freedom through business ownership. I felt like little Simba. I was ready to become the Lion King!

Around this same period in my life, I decided to establish a relationship with God, and I wanted to study and learn the Bible.

I decided to enroll in a Tuesday night Bible study at my church. One night, while at the Bible study I fell sound asleep. I mean, I wasn't just sleeping, I was knocked out! Mouth open and everything! Not because of a lack of interest, but because of extreme fatigue from work. Here you have what many would argue to be the most important thing in life... having a spiritual connection with God, yet, I was being hindered because I was doing as I was told and working my life away at my "good job."

I began to think about my future, and where I was headed and wondered, If I were married, would I have time to spend with my wife? I knew that I wanted kids, but would I have the ability to rear them properly? Would I be able to spend time with them, or would my life be like the one of Adam Sandler in the movie "Click," and I'd miss my kids' swim meets or other activities? Would vacations have to be put off to make an important meeting to please my boss, but disappoint my family? What if a close relative died, and all my sick days were gone? Would I possibly lose my job, or have my pay docked? All of these things were racing through my head. There were many people that I knew that lived their lives this way, seeking the almighty dollar. That won't be me, I thought. This could not be my purpose in life. I knew it. I also knew that there had to be more to life than working just to make money to buy stuff. There had to be a greater purpose for my life!

# THREE

# A Contrapreneur Is Born

---

"Jerome has written a simple, yet powerful book that is destined to bring out the contrapreneur in all of us."

**—ReShonda Tate Billingsley, National Bestselling Author**

Upon having this disheartening experience I made up in my mind there had to be a change. It was then that I began down a path to start my own business or to find a job that would allow me more freedom. Fast forward a year or so, after my junior year in college, and graduation was just around the corner. Since it was almost graduation time, and the financial support of my parents would soon be gone, the pressure was on. I only had about a year and a half to make a decision on what path my life would take from that point.

In May of 1998, during a trip to Houston, Texas, the course of my life was drastically altered. I went to Houston one weekend to hang out with one of my fraternity brothers. While there, I decided to call some of my family members that lived in the area. As we spoke, one of my aunts, told me that I had picked a good time to come to town, as one of our cousins, Derrick Love, was graduating that weekend.

Derrick was the son of my Dad's second oldest brother. I knew who he was, but at that point I had only seen him three times in my life, with the last time being when we both lived in Louisiana in 1986.

After the graduation, I remember greeting Derrick for the first time in more than 10 years. The last time I saw him he was this short, stocky little fellow and now, he was as tall as I was. He had on a red graduation robe and he was grinning from ear to ear. This was his big day. Everyone decided to go out for a bite to eat at a local restaurant afterward, and as fate would have it, I ended up riding with Derrick.

Although we had not seen each other for a decade, we immediately connected. We talked about life and being financially independent. It was at that time that Derrick told me about a concept that he had come up with called GUGOGS: Get Up, Get Out, Get Something. I asked what he was going to do with it, and he told me that he didn't know. He showed me a few drawings of some bracelet designs, similar to the popular W.W.J.D. (What Would Jesus Do) bands, but he said that he was open to my suggestions. The concept was catchy, and the idea was brilliant. I felt as though this was my big opportunity to break into the world of being a business owner and get the heck away from my day job!

Derrick and I talked about moving forward, but shortly after his graduation in May, he joined the Navy and left the country on an extended tour.

With Derrick's blessing, I now had this great concept, but I still had to figure out what to do with it. The first thing I did was to take the idea to Alejandro Vasquez, my fraternity brother who owned a t-shirt and embroidery shop.

> In order to be truly successful, you must build a business that is systems-driven and not create a job that is driven by you and your labor.

Alejandro was a kindred spirit. He, too went to The University of Texas at Austin and was being groomed to climb the corporate ladder. Like me, he felt that corporate life was not for him and he decided to start his own business. Eventually, his shop would grow to be one of the largest shops in Austin, with branches throughout Texas.

Since he had a t-shirt shop, the simplest and easiest thing for me to do was to print some t-shirts and start a clothing line, at least I thought. Alejandro had one of his designers create a logo for me. My first logo was this oval shaped design with "GUGOGS" written in lower case in the center. Just below that were the words "Get up, Get out, Get something." It was perfect. I persuaded Alejandro to print 12 shirts for me on credit, and I promised to pay him as soon as I sold them. With that, I was off to become a mercantile millionaire. Or so I thought!

My first three shirt styles became known as the GUGOGS original logo. We had the logo in red and white on a black t-shirt, blue and white on a gray shirt, and mint green and white on a navy shirt. They were beautiful. I began wearing these shirts every day all over the University of Texas at Austin campus. I also gave a few to some of my fraternity brothers. The very first day, people began asking questions about the shirt and commenting on how they liked it. I would proudly tell them this is my new clothing line. Within a few weeks, it began to catch on like wildfire! As with many colleges, at UT Austin, fraternities and sororities were major parts of campus life. As a result, the majority of my sales were to the various fraternities and sororities. They each were placing bulk orders in their particular groups' traditional colors. Before I knew it, I was getting requests for other items such as hats, women's baby tees, long sleeve shirts, etc.

Within a couple of months, I was selling, on average 10 to 15 shirts a week at $15 a pop. I had expanded from the three different styles of t-shirts with the original logo to include baby tees, hats, long sleeve shirts, and any other items that people requested. I even created my own GUGOGS website! Business was booming, and I just knew that Footlocker or a major chain would soon be calling, begging me to carry GUGOGS. After all, I had sold close to 400 shirts. I was famous (at least in my mind)!

Sales were consistent with GUGOGS, so to me, things were going well. Now, taking a step back to analyze the situation, the truth was that I really wasn't making much money. After manufacturing costs, there was very little profit. For instance, if a shirt sold for $15, I actually made approximately $8 in profit. I soon realized that by placing larger orders, I could reduce product cost to almost $3.50. So I began to think of ways to expand and sell more shirts in order to produce more profit.

My first thought was to become a vendor at different tradeshows and conventions. Through these arenas, I could purchase an exhibit space for roughly $600, a minor investment for the opportunity to reach thousands of potential customers, right? So I decided to give it a try.

Fast forward another eight months to my first convention, which was the Alpha Phi Alpha Fraternity national convention in Dallas, Texas in 1999. I shared a booth with one of my best friends, Aaron Terry, who, at the time, had launched his own business creating artistic poetry. It was a four-day convention that started on a Thursday. I went in, never having exhibited before at a tradeshow. Therefore, I was not as prepared as other vendors. They had all kinds of mannequins and other elaborate displays. I remember seeing people with fancy shelves and product neatly stacked and arranged in pyramids or some other unique, eye-catching shape. The clothing vendors had their clothing on racks, and hanging neatly on the back wall, and had strategically located displays.

Although, many of their displays were more eye-catching than mine, I remained confident. I arrogantly thought that this magnificent concept and design would definitely sell itself. After all, I had already sold 400 shirts.

At the end of the first day, I was severely disappointed when Aaron had 10 to 15 poems sold and I had a big fat ZERO shirts sold. I bring up Aaron's sales simply to illustrate the fact that people were buying stuff, just not mine!

That night, Aaron and I went to Home Depot and bought some display items to spice up the display. I was a bit frustrated while walking down the aisles of Home Depot on sore feet from a full day of working the tradeshow. As I walked, a million things ran through my mind - most of which were negative, and that only made me more depressed. Did I waste my money on this show? Maybe I wasn't cut out to be in business on my own. Maybe working in corporate America was where I belonged. I thought of all the potentially negative outcomes. I needed to figure out how to deal with the reality that I didn't know what to do. Having a business was new to me, and so far, I wasn't knocking the ball out of the park.

The second day, Aaron and I decided to show up early to fix up the exhibit display. If we were going to attract more customers, our booth needed a serious overhaul. We purchased five six-foot chains and hooks, which hung on the back draping. We then used two to three-foot sticks to hang the shirts displaying the logo. It definitely made a big difference in making the display look better.

Throughout the day, I gave potential customers my best spiel on GUGOGS. The majority responded, "Maybe later", or "I'll be back tomorrow."

There were some that used the good ol' "I left my money or checkbook in the hotel room" trick. The most aggravating of them all was what I call the "Stingy Encourager." Those were the folks that would stand in front of my booth for what seemed like hours. They'd say how great the idea was, commenting on how professional it looked. Then, they'd ask questions as to how I came up with this brilliant idea, only to then encourage me with, "Best of luck," without spending a dime. You also had the "Whipped Warriors." These were the guys that would come by, sing my praises, tell me that they really liked my stuff and tell me how much they really wanted to buy, but they needed to check with their wives first.

As Day Two came to a close, much to my dismay, I had sold a staggering three shirts, and made a measly $45. I went home completely discouraged, feeling like I had just wasted my money on the convention, the inventory, and not to mention the last six to eight months of my life trying to build a clothing line that was obviously doomed. I remember sharing my frustrations with Aaron and saying, "I guess I'll have to do something else."

Then came Day Three. Although discouraged, I figured that my money was already spent on this convention, I might as well make the best out of it. I really couldn't think of anything else new to say, so I went with my same spiel from the previous days. It went something like this: When spotting a person to pitch, I would ask the question, "Have you ever heard of GUGOGS?" - a question to which the answer I already knew. Most would say "GUGOGS? What is that?" or "Huh, Googles, what?"

I'd then repeat the name "GUGOGS." Then I would say, "Well, come over here and let me tell you about it." Then I would explain the meaning behind the acronym and how it was meant to motivate people to strive for greatness. Well, wouldn't you know it: Day Three was my lucky day! At the end of that day, I had sold somewhere in the neighborhood of 65 shirts! I was thrilled. Not only had I made my money back, but I made a bit of profit. So, I figured I was set, even if I bombed again on Day Four.

Things just kept looking up. At the end of Day Four, I had sold 95 shirts and depleted my inventory! Day Four was great, and sales were constant. People were standing in line to buy my stuff! I couldn't believe it. What was even better than that was the fact that people that bought shirts on previous days were wearing them that day and had become walking billboards for me!

Later, I was told that there had been a fraternity party the night before. At that party, there were upwards of 20 to 30 people wearing my shirts. It created a tremendous buzz and resulted in folks clamoring for GUGOGS apparel. Amazingly, people just couldn't get enough of GUGOGS!

For every objection that I'd faced, I had the right answer to make the sale. I remember frantically rummaging through boxcs looking for a small or medium, as stock was running low, but demand was at an all-time high! I recall the great feeling that came over me as I began taking shirts off of the display wall to sell. I will never forget that feeling as I began to pack up at the end of the tradeshow and I was left with an empty box. That was one of the greatest feelings I have ever experienced in my entire life! I was grinning from ear to ear and brimming with confidence. It had been a great day for GUGOGS!

Over the next year or so, I exhibited at different conventions and tradeshows on a regular basis, averaging $2,000 to $3,000 per event. My best convention was the National Society of Black Engineers national convention in Charlotte, North Carolina where I brought in just short of $5,000. While this was better cash flow than I'd had previously, somehow my bank account always seemed to be a little short. I had what we now call "funny money."

Thinking back, it was very simple to figure out. The cost for each show was approximately $500. Travel and meals were roughly $400, depending upon proximity, and supply cost was about 40 percent of the revenue. So, you do the math. If I made $3,000, 40 percent of that is $1,200. Then, you add in the other costs and I was left with $1,100. Keep in mind that there was another show the following month, for which I had to pay another registration fee plus inventory. So, you know what that means, right? No money for Jerome. Not yet anyway.

Fast forward another few months to August 1999, prior to my final semester in college. It was around this time that Alejandro told me about a major show that took place twice annually in Las Vegas called The Magic Show. He and one of his designers were considering putting together a clothing line, and he suggested that we check it out. The Magic Show, as he explained, was where all the major names in the fashion industry were. It was a must for any serious clothing line. So, I did a little research online and decided that I would visit the Fall show with Alejandro, which was held every September.

I took a week off of school and went to Vegas. This was by far the largest tradeshow I'd ever been to, and needless to say, I was blown away.

The Magic Show was so big that it needed not one, but two entire convention centers. It was everything I had imagined plus much, much more. I remember walking in like a kid in a candy store. There were booths that were two and even three stories high! There were banners hanging from rafters everywhere. There were exhibits designed to look like playgrounds with kids wear, or a basketball court for athletic apparel. Still, others had built coffee shops. Some had stages with live performances. I'd never seen anything like this before! There were 3,000 plus exhibitors and hundreds of thousands of attendees. All of the major buyers were there, including big names such as Footlocker and The Gap.

In addition, all of the major clothing lines such as Tommy Hilfiger and Ralph Lauren were there, among many others. Additionally, many of the major celebrity designers such as Russell Simmons, Master P, Shaquille O'Neal and Hugh Heffner were present. On the shuttle bus, I met a distributor from Aruba who placed a $1,500 order with me!

Needless to say, when I got back to Texas the first thing on my agenda was to register for the next Magic Show to be held in the Spring. I thought that I'd clean up, especially since my line was leaps and bounds above anything there. There was just one small problem. The registration fee for Magic at the time was $3,000 for a 10X10 booth space. I also found that, unlike other shows I had been to, they didn't allow pipe and drape booths. They required custom hard-wall designed booths, which would cost another $3,000. Add the freight charges of getting the booth from Texas to Las Vegas and you got another $700. And let's not forget about the other marketing costs: flyers, models, inventory and other collateral materials. Not including our travel, we were looking at total damage of about $16,000.

Rather than view this as an obstacle, I figured that if I could just make it there, I'd be fine. Alejandro, another local designer, and myself partnered and decided we'd get five booths together in an attempt to not get lost with all of the other larger-than-life exhibits. This really wouldn't reduce my cost much, but in my mind, I had calculated that I'd come back with at least a $20,000 in orders. If I could land a deal (which I had already on the shuttle bus at the Fall show) without having a booth, surely, I reasoned, success was inevitable now that we were exhibiting.

I then began to seek out sources of funding and found a non-profit organization that specialized in funding small businesses. I submitted my business plan, and lo and behold I was approved for a loan in the amount of $20,000!

Assuming that this was a sign from above, I was so gung ho that I never questioned whether this was the right decision.

In December 1999, I signed the loan documents a week after graduation from college. The next month-and-a-half was spent working on a booth design, which, for me, was characterized by frustration. I was the guy who wanted everything done yesterday, and tended to be a bit impatient. Since the designer was one of Alejandro's friends, and Jason, the one that would build the booth, was a friend of the other guy we partnered with, I had little control. We met every night in east Austin at this little shop to work on our booths. During these times, we bonded and shared dreams of making it big at the Magic Show.

Looking back, it was a fun time, and I realize many of the things that worried me really didn't amount to much of anything.

The Spring Magic Show was to be held in mid February of

2000, and we were running a bit behind schedule. The week before the show, we were about 70 percent complete, and of the 30 percent that remained to be done, the majority was on my booth. At least it seemed that way to me.

Although the booths were not complete, we had to pack up and get everything to Vegas. To keep costs down, we rented a huge U-Haul truck and drove our booths to Las Vegas. Alejandro and Jason were the designated drivers, and they set out on Thursday prior to the show, which was scheduled to start on the following Tuesday.

We arrived on Saturday and got settled in. After I made my way over to the convention center, I saw something that left me in shock. The convention hall looked completely different from when I had visited previously. This hall, which had previously been filled with elaborate displays and celebrities galore, was now characterized by the smell of sawdust and the sound of forklifts zooming by in preparation for the coming show. It was as though they were building a mini city. I anxiously pulled out my floor plan to locate our booth to see what it looked like, only to be disappointed to find an empty piece of concrete with tape around it, outlining where our booth would be. It looked like a scene right out of an episode of CSI.

Next to the booth I found Alejandro and Jason. They explained that they were not allowed to bring the booth into the building. They had to check it in with the decorator, who then would deliver the booth to our space. At this point in my life, I had not yet learned the art of diplomacy, and I began to vent my frustration. Not only was my booth seemingly the only one that was incomplete, but it was also two days until show time and no one else seemed to have any sense of urgency.

Alejandro, who was masterful at dealing with people, then came to me and gently told me to go back to the hotel room, so not to further upset the guys responsible for building the booth. I reluctantly agreed and went back to the hotel. The majority of the next two days for me was spent in the casino trying to take my mind off of worrying.

The day prior to the show, my cousin Derrick, Aaron, and my broker Byron arrived in town, along with the six models that I flew in from Austin. We all went to dinner that night and I gave them all a rundown on the next day's activities. After dinner, I made my first trip back to the convention center, only to find a partially completed booth. My frustration mounted, so I just went back to the hotel and didn't say a word for fear of saying the wrong thing.

Tuesday morning, it was show time. I woke up early that morning, as I couldn't sleep with all of the anxiety. My cousin Derrick, Aaron and I caught a shuttle to the convention center and arrived around 6:45 a.m., with the doors set to open at 8:00. We were all dressed in red polo shirts, with a blue and white GUGOGS logo embroidered on the left side. We had these shirts specially made for the show.

Once arriving at the booth, I immediately noticed that they had worked a bit on the booth, but it was still far from complete. The structure of the booth was up so we could exhibit, but our logo was not adorned on the back wall as it was supposed to be. Feeling as though it would only increase frustrations, I didn't say anything, as now it was 8:00 am and the show had started.

Jason showed up shortly after the show began and started to work on completing our booth design. He worked, while I was inundated with the thousands of people that seemed to come from nowhere. It was a bit overwhelming, and I wasn't prepared for it. The people were moving so fast, and the show was so big I really wasn't able to pitch very many people.

In addition, the environment was a lot more hostile than I was accustomed to. The other vendors were not very friendly, as they viewed us as their competitor. One even threatened one of my models because she handed a flyer to someone that he felt was about to come to his booth. It was a long day that I was glad to see end, even though we didn't have any orders.

On Wednesday, I woke up with a new zeal and was ready to make some sales. Jason had completed the booth design that previous night after the show closed, so I knew that with the completed design in my arsenal, our fortunes would change. Upon arrival at the convention center, we went through the same routine as the previous day, which consisted of getting a snack before reporting to our booth. Day Two was even more overwhelming than the previous day. There were more people, and it was hard to keep up. In addition, on Day Two we had another incident with the exhibitor across from us. They decided to bring in people to break dance in front of their booth in order to attract a crowd. Unfortunately, it worked… they attracted a crowd, but it was the wrong type of crowd… a crowd comprised of mostly spectators.

Due to the large crowds and huge traffic jam on our aisle, many serious buyers were skipping our row so they didn't have to deal with the crowd. It would have been okay if they'd only had one performance, but they had one almost every hour, or so it seemed. As a result, I had to have a heated conversation with the exhibitor and threaten to call management if the performances didn't stop.

Although Day Two was frustrating, we somehow had managed to land our first buyer, a small store in Illinois that ordered about $1,500 in clothing.

Thursday and Friday went by so quickly that they seemed to be one short day. A short day that was summed up in two words: fatigue and frustration. We were fatigued as a result of working on our feet 10 straight hours a day, trying to solicit everyone that went by. Consequently, by the end of each day, we were so tired, and our feet were so sore that we could barely make the five to six block walk to catch the shuttle back to the hotel. We were frustrated because although we'd given it our best shot, it seemed like our best had not been good enough.

Over those two days, we had accumulated another $6,000 in orders, but that was far short of the $20,000 goal. In addition, the orders were all being paid on net 30 or 60 terms. In other words, we would not get our money until 30 to 60 days after receipt of product.

I began to review the big picture. I'd just spent $16,000 to do the show, acquiring a monthly loan payment of $356 had been in the process. I also had to come up with another $3,000 to $4,000 to fill the orders. Things were not looking good for GUGOGS. I ended up using the rest of the bank money to fill the orders. In addition, I went to New York to exhibit at another tradeshow that recruited me at Magic, which only put me further in the hole.

I returned to Texas broke and in debt. That's when I began to work full-time selling real estate to pay back the loan and to cover my living expenses.

By that time, I was out of college, and my parental support was gone. Even while working in real estate, in the back of my mind, I thought it was just temporary, and I would get back to GUGOGS sooner or later. However, my passion never came back. Even though I continued to do tradeshows for a while, it was no longer fun and exciting. It was just a job. With no passion and no excitement, my business died.

This was my baptism by fire into the world of owning a business. Although it was a rough time, I am appreciative of everything that I experienced. It is because of what I experienced that I am where I am today.

After putting GUGOGS to sleep, I moved on to start a number of businesses that have been very successful; the most notable being the Houston Black Expo, which is one of the largest consumer tradeshows in the country.

Through the process, I have learned the importance of thinking outside the box and not trying to be like everyone else. This is the essence of Contrapreneurship!

Contrapreneurship is a lifestyle. It is a way of thinking that opposes tradition. It's the future of business as we know it. By learning and embracing the principles of contrapreneurship, you will be light years ahead of the average business owner. You will also avoid many of the costly mistakes that I had to learn the hard way. My hard knocks lessons can be your stepping-stones to success.

# FOUR

# Conceive A Business...Not A Job

---

"Jerome hasn't just written a laundry list of steps to starting a business, he has lived and modeled every one of the principles set forth in his book. His energetic and proactive approach to business has inspired me and many others to pursue our business goals."

**— Anastasia Gentles, M.D., CEO Nightlight Afterhour Pediatrics**

Once upon a time, there was a small village, and this village had a problem. A big problem. They were located about a quarter of a mile away from the mainland, which was separated by a lake. The mainland was where the majority of the businesses, grocery stores and jobs were located. Thus, in order for the villagers to get to the mainland, they had to swim, as many could not afford boats. Swimming was the only real option, even though it was very tiring and took an extra hour of the people's time.

One day, the village elders decided to get together to solve the problem, and they decided to hire two people to fix the problem. One was your average entrepreneur while the other was a contrapreneur.

The entrepreneur took the money that he had saved from other business ventures and bought a state-of-the-art-ferry. Within a week, he launched his new business, "The Entrepreneur's Ferry Service."

Business was booming, as he had come up with a solution to a very big problem. His state of the art ferry could carry up to eight villagers at a time, including the operator. In order for the ferry to move, the owner would have to peddle as fast as he could, which would propel the ferry forward. The total round trip took half an hour, and a round trip ticket was $1.

The entrepreneur's hours of operation were Monday through Friday from 8 a.m. to 5 p.m. If you take out the hour lunch break and the 10-minute breaks needed after each round trip, he was able to actually work a total of seven hours, which meant 14 daily trips. Fourteen daily trips with seven passengers paying $1 dollar per trip meant $98 per day. Although he came home each day exhausted from peddling his little ferry all day long, he was happy, because he had his own business and it was bringing in a hefty $98 a day; a sum that, at the time, was nothing to sneeze at.

While the entrepreneur worked his ferry business, the contrapreneur disappeared for a few months, wrote a business plan, found some investors, hired a construction crew, and came back to build a toll bridge. Villagers had the opportunity to travel across this bridge 24 hours a day, seven days a week at a nominal fee of $.75 per trip, or $1.50 for a round trip ticket.

The contrapreneur's toll bridge averaged a total of 50 round trip tickets an hour, which meant a daily income of $1,800. The contrapreneur had created a bridge that made him more than eighteen times what the entrepreneur made, without any manual labor!

In an attempt to compete with the contrapreneur, the entrepreneur bought a trailer hitch for his ferry that carried four additional villagers, cut his lunch, and extended his hours from

8 a.m. to 5 p.m. to 6 a.m. to 6 p.m. This allowed him to add eight additional trips a day in order to carry more villagers, which increased his daily income to $154. He also began to work on weekends in an attempt to keep up with the contrapreneur. Thus, his income increased a little, but his workload more than doubled.

The contrapreneur, on the other hand, went to all the other surrounding villages that had similar problems, rewrote his business plan, and sold his bridge system to all the other villages in exchange for a quarter per round trip. Sure, it was less than what he was making at his village, but he now had the capacity to sell billions of tickets daily, whether he worked or not. He owned a business, and as a result, it operated independently of him. He had built a system that deposited money into his pocket without very much involvement from him.

In contrast, the entrepreneur had created himself a perpetual job. In order to increase his income, he had to work more hours while carrying a heavier load each time. He was always tired and never seemed to be able to get ahead financially.

The contrapreneur lived happily ever after, and when he died, his family still received the financial benefits of the system that he built. The entrepreneur, on the other hand, was divorced by his wife because he never spent time with her. He had a heart attack and died early from the stress and pressure, and his children didn't want the family business, because they saw how much stress it had put on their father. As a result, when he died, the company died with him. On the other hand, the contrapreneur's company revenues increased. Why? Well, for starters, the dead entrepreneur's clients began to travel on his toll bridge.

The moral of the story?

In order to be truly successful, you must build a business that is systems-driven and not create a job that is driven by you and your labor. You may be able to generate a ton of money for a while, but what happens if you can't work? In addition, what kind of lifestyle are you leading while you're making all of this money?

The entrepreneur had a desire to make money, but he didn't think about the long-term ramifications. The contrapreneur, meanwhile, realized that he would never have the type of lifestyle that he enjoyed by personally carrying people back and forth over the lake, so he created a system that would run independent of him.

All contrapreneurs understand that the truly successful business owner seeks not to do all the work by themselves, but to create an enterprise that can operate at full tilt, even if he's in Italy sipping on fine wine or eating a hearty bowl of fettuccine!

Which one of these people closest resembles you? Are you still toting people back and forth across the water, or are you building bridges?

# FIVE

# Consult with an Advisor

---

"Contrapreneurship is essential reading for anyone who wants to have a successful business & create a lifestyle they love. Jerome Love has done it again!"

**—Jonathan Sprinkles, APCA National Speaker of the Year**

Before going to the Magic Show, I was pumped about the potential of my business. In my head was a map of some of the marketing plan, which, of course included attending the now infamous Magic Show.

Prior to getting approved for my business loan, I went to a local Chamber of Commerce where they gave me the name of a potential investor by the name of Dr. Norman Mason. He was a very successful businessman and dentist in Austin, Texas. He was a very wise man and obviously very successful, so I decided to talk to him to get his advice on whether to take the loan and to get his perspective on the business in general. Although I was asking for his advice and insight into my business, I also wanted to get validation that I was making a smart move. Validation that I wasn't completely losing my mind.

As I drove through the rolling hills of his exclusive neighborhood, it was clear that this meeting would be a defining moment on my contrapreneurial journey. I remember rehearsing my "elevator" pitch in the car. The elevator pitch, in case you're not familiar, is that quick business synopsis that all of the gurus tell you that you need to have in your back pocket ready to pull out on a moment's notice. I went through my presentation one last time, and then got out of the car. Before ringing the doorbell I took a deep breath. Whatever awaited me on the other side was all good, I was sure of it.

The custom cherry wood doors looked bigger than they were, but when you're nervous, things tend to take on a life of their own, and those doors were no exception. Dr. Mason greeted me and led me into his living room.

"Can I get you anything to drink?" he asked.

Drink? There was no way I could even think about drinking anything. I was anxious to share my vision and plan, and even though they tell you in Business Etiquette 101 to always accept the host's offer of drink or food, all I could think of was getting down to business.

"I'm planning to take out a $20,000 loan to finance GUGOGS," I told him after he was seated. He nodded and listened intently, hanging on to my every word. I was talking a mile a minute, excited by the prospect of getting my first "real" business loan and thrilled that a man of Dr. Mason's reputation and affluence was interested in me and my future.

When I finally slowed down to take a breath, Dr. Mason chimed in. "Jerome, GUGOGS is a great idea. It really is," he said. "But right now, you're operating more out of passion rather than a plan."

What he said next was somewhat prophetic. I knew it needed to be said, but wasn't sure I wanted to hear it.

"You are about to go out there, get yourself in a lot of debt, then come back and have to work a job to pay off the debt, and it will kill your business," he said. "And I don't think you're ready for The Magic Show."

My heart sank. Not ready? Not ready? I felt like Rod Tidwell, Cuba Gooding, Jr.'s character in the movie Jerry Maguire when Tom Cruise's character told him, "You got no heart." The PG version of the movie has Rod saying, "I'm all heart, my brother!" As I sat there listening to Dr. Mason, I felt Rod's pain. I wanted to say, "I am ready! I'm so ready!"

Shocked by his response, I immediately launched back into motormouth mode, re-explaining the idea and concept, because surely, I reasoned, he's not seeing the full picture. He doesn't see how huge this thing's gonna be. He must have misunderstood me. So I continued to talk. And talk. And talk. I was trying to convince him that he was wrong, and I was right.

Finally, he leaned forward, looked me dead in the eyes and said, "Jerome, what's the point of having access to someone like me if you're not going to listen?"

Wow. He was right. I'd felt so grateful to be able to get the meeting with him, but I quickly realized that the only reason I was excited was because I knew he'd see things my way, pat me on the back, and maybe even cut a big fat check! Boy, did I have a lot to learn!

What Dr. Mason gave me was exactly what was needed. Sage advice and sound business counsel from a man who'd been there and gotten the t-shirt.

So, where's your lesson in my story? As a business owner, you'll be faced with many challenges on a daily basis. You'll be

> In business it is important to realize that there is nothing new under the sun. Any problem that you may face has already been faced by hundreds of business owners before you.

faced with a number of obstacles, dilemmas and questions to which you will not know the answers. Plus, many times, there won't be a clear or right answer. As a contrapreneur, you have to be an innovator, a visionary, a creator. Therefore, many of the situations you face will require you to play it by ear. You have to snap out of that employee mindset of being told what to do and learn to make decisions on your own.

In business, it is important to realize that there is nothing new under the sun. Any problem that you may face has already been faced by thousands of business owners before you. It could be that you need to know how to generate funds for your business. You may have questions about which corporate structure is right for you, or how to find the right employees. The concerns and questions that business owners face are numerous, and if you want to be successful, you will eventually need to consult with an advisor or someone who has experienced what you're going through.

There are lots of seasoned business owners and business advisors out there that could help you navigate through some of these situations. It's imperative that you not allow your ego, pride, or fear to keep you from the knowledge that can transform your business. Many of these people may even be willing to work with you for free. I wouldn't necessarily expect to get free advice, but I've found that when you approach people with the right attitude, they're often quite generous with their time and resources.

Others may charge you a consulting fee, and you have to determine for yourself whether or not it's worth it. You have to decide if the return that you will receive from the investment of advice will warrant the expense. I'm a big believer in outside consulting, and I know that my business has grown by leaps and bounds because of the insights I've gotten from other business owners or consultants.

Choosing an advisor is an important step in your business. Before you decide on one though, ask yourself if the person appears to be a giver or a taker. Have they attempted to take from you without first making a deposit?

Had I interviewed my advisors just as they had been interviewing me, I would have saved myself a lot of money and heartache. I met a lot of people who were more experienced and knowledgeable and wanted to "help" me with my tradeshow business. Yet, upon gaining my confidence, I found them to do more taking than giving. They were constantly reminding me of how they were helping me, but in reality they were playing on my youth and lack of confidence.

For example, when speaking with Dr. Mason about GUGOGS, he began to tell me about how he'd wasted a lot of money in the music business when he was "young and dumb."

He was attempting to convey that when you're young and eager, sometimes you don't think straight. But because I was so intoxicated with emotions and arrogance, I couldn't appreciate what he was saying at the time. I thought, "What in the world does his musical group have to do with GUGOGS?"

Looking back, it is evident that Dr. Mason was trying to stop me from making the same mistakes he had made. He was trying to get me to stop operating out of passion and instead, develop a plan. Sometimes we have to learn lessons the hard way.

> To grow your business, though, you must be able to take a step back and see it from many different perspectives. And if you don't have the ability to bring that objectivity to your business, an advisor or coach becomes even more critical to your success.

Sometimes we get so wrapped up in situations and circumstances that our emotions prevent us from seeing the whole picture. It's like the saying, "You can't see the forest for the trees." There are some things that you can't see but are obvious to others. The best example I can give illustrating this is in the game of basketball. One of the greatest teams to ever play, in my opinion, was the Chicago Bulls of the '90's, under the leadership of Hall of Fame Coach Phil Jackson. Of course, the leader on the team was one of the most dynamic players of all time, Michael Jordan.

Here you have a Hall of Fame coach and a future Hall of Fame player, who by all accounts were two of the greatest the game has ever known. Yet, there were many situations where Phil Jackson or Michael Jordan received technical fouls for arguing with the referee over calls made during the game.

Now, while the calls may have been obvious to the millions of viewers at home or to a neutral fan in the crowd, to Jackson or Jordan the calls were often bogus. They'd gotten so caught up in the game, so driven by their emotions, that sometimes they couldn't see clear violations of simple rules.

Or let's look at a different scenario. Let's say the Bulls are down by one point, with 10 seconds to go in the game, and Jordan is driving to the basket. He misses the shot, and the buzzer sounds, but he thinks he's fouled. The official doesn't make the call, and the New York Knicks win. Who's right? Is Jordan right?

Did he get fouled? Maybe. Is the Knicks player right by saying he didn't touch Jordan? Or is the official who made the call truly an objective party to the scene?

Ideally, the official is supposed to be that objective voice that provides balance in a sometimes unbalanced situation. Well, that's the same role that mentors can sometimes play on your contrapreneurial journey. Sometimes, you may not agree with the calls your advisors make, but a good businessman knows the value of having an outside opinion.

Your business is your baby, so you can't help but be emotionally attached to it. That's fine. There's nothing wrong with that. To grow your business, though, you must be able to take a step back and see it from many different perspectives. If you don't have the ability to bring that objectivity to your business, an advisor or coach becomes even more critical to your success.

The question then is, How do I get a mentor or advisor, and who should I choose to be my mentor? I believe that there are two basic types of mentors, which are formal and informal mentors.

## FORMAL MENTORS

Formal mentors may be individuals that you don't know or you don't know that well. You may seek them out for the sole purpose of mentorship, because you perceive him or her to be in a position that you hope to be in one day. Let's say that you want to start a nonprofit organization that helps people find homes and fights predatory lending. The first thing you should do is to research similar companies or organizations.

These organizations don't have to have the same mission or agenda as your company, but they should be similar in terms of the services they provide. The next step might be to call the President or Executive Director of that organization and ask for a meeting. Keep in mind, most successful business people will be very busy, so don't get frustrated if you have to leave several messages. Be persistent.

At that first meeting or in that first phone conversation, be honest with the potential mentor. Say something along the lines of, "I really admire what you've accomplished. I'd like to learn from you. One day I hope to follow in your footsteps and build a successful company in the industry."

Be direct. Don't expect someone to deduce from the previous statement that you'd like for him or her to mentor you. Ask for the sale, as we say in the sales industry. "Would you consider being my mentor?"

If you get a positive response, be ready to provide some ideas about how you see the relationship playing out. Remember, there are no set rules for mentoring relationships. Some involve monthly contact, others weekly. It's up to you and your mentor. The key is for both of you to have a clear understanding of the framework of your relationship. The last thing you want is for the mentor to think one thing, yet you have a completely different expectation. Communication is clearly of absolute importance.

Taking my own advice I sought out a mentor to teach me how to produce a successful expo or tradeshow. The Houston Black Expo was conceived in 2002, and we had our first Expo in May of 2004. After the 2004 event, I continued my research and ultimately found the Indiana Black Expo, the largest black expo in the country. It boasts more than 300,000 total attendees annually and has a total economic impact of $72.6 million on its local economy. It looked like a great model for the Houston Black

Expo. I didn't hesitate. I learned a long time ago that if you want to be the best in your field, you have to study the best.

So for that reason, I picked up the phone and called their president. I told her how impressive her organization and their accomplishments were, and that our company wanted to be like theirs one day. She was very kind and generous with her information and invited me to see the Indiana Black Expo "in action." In July of 2006, I flew to Indiana. The staff was very hospitable, and they treated me like royalty. They gave me VIP tickets to everything, limo transportation to various events, and I had a chance to see them "do their thing" up close and personal. I also had the pleasure of speaking with one of their original members who started with them in 1972. It was awesome.

Not only did I get a chance to see their operations in person, but afterward, they sent me their chapter manual and annual report. All of this came about because I wasn't afraid to pick up the phone and ask for help. As a result, I've built a relationship with the Indiana Black Expo team. We share ideas and resources that continue to build our respective businesses. So you see, what started out as me reaching out for support has resulted in clear, sustainable, and measurable outcomes in which both parties win. That's the power of mentoring relationships.

## INFORMAL MENTORS

Informal mentors are people who share sound advice and relevant experiences with you. With informal mentors, you have the freedom to call them up and ask for advice as needed. People who fall into this category could be business associates, your pastor, friends or family members that bring knowledge or expertise to your project or business. These are people with whom you have an established relationship. You don't necessarily have to ask them to be your mentor; because they have often fallen naturally into that role.

I am fortunate to have what is one of the best informal mentors on the planet, my pastor, Dr. Dana Carson. He's very knowledgeable in terms of practical everyday advice, but he's also earned several doctorate degrees, including one in leadership organization. He has been a pastor since 1986 and has built several successful businesses in the restaurant and coffee industries. He's a true inspiration, and I value him and his business expertise very much.

The great thing about informal mentors is that they know you personally. Consequently, not only do they have the ability to advise you on the proper business decisions, they can also help you to determine some of your character flaws that may be counterproductive to your business' success.

You have to find yourself a mentor, or an advisor! They can be critical to the growth and development of your business. Many of the world's best and brightest minds credit their success to mentors. Take for example, Warren Buffet. Buffett is widely regarded by many as being the greatest investor of all time. In the book Warren Buffett Speaks by Janet Lowe, Buffett is quoted as saying, "Next to my Dad, Ben Graham had more impact certainly on my business life than any individual."

Well, who is Ben Graham you may ask? Ben Graham was Buffett's mentor. Buffett's first introduction with Graham was when he read his book, The Intelligent Investor, which Buffett celebrates as, "the greatest book on investing ever." He later studied under Graham at Colombia University, and upon graduation went on to work for Graham. They built a strong relationship, a relationship that resulted in Warren Buffett becoming a multibillionaire and one of the greatest investors that the world has known.

I'll say it one more time, a mentor is critical to you succeeding in your business.

However, watch out, there's another type of mentor out there as well, but following their counsel will have a negative effect. I call these people "Tormentors." See if you know anyone who fits into one of these categories.

## TORMENTOR #1

The first category of tormentors includes the people that drain the life out of you with their negative words and negative actions. They're the people that you call to discuss your day with, but somehow you always end up listening to their sob story! Negativity is always a choice. They have a choice to be negative, and you have a choice to hang around them and their negativity.

The most important thing to note is that negative people typically desire to contaminate everything and everyone around them. In other words, if you are in their presence they will do their best to bring you down with them.

For example, if you say, "It's a beautiful day outside," they'll always remind you of the possibility of rain.

When you are around a Category 1 Tormentor and you're excited and happy about your new business, they will immediately think of ways to bring you down. And in your lowest moment, when you really need an encouraging word, they'll be right there to spew negativity in your ear.

Their negative words will become lodged in your subconscious mind and will manifest in you to the point that you become even more negative or depressed.

Remember: what you nurture grows! Fertilize negativity, and that's what will grow in your business garden. Fertilize positive energy, and you'll manifest positive results.

## TORMENTOR #2

Category 2 Tormentors, if left unwatched, can wreak just as much havoc and torment on your business, plus, by following their advice you'll never succeed as a business owner.

These tormentors often offer bad counsel and also typically

bring a low level of knowledge in a particular area and a high level of emotional attachment to you. They offer advice based on emotional reasoning, which may pacify the immediate distress but could also cause long term negative ramifications. What I'm saying is that all advice is not good advice.

## JUST SAY "NO"

I have never really asked my parents for advice in the area of business, yet through conversations we've had, I have a definite idea of where they stand on certain issues. I remember talking to my mom about my business endeavors and goals, and she responded with, "That's too much work. I'd rather have someone else take care of me."

Mom began to share all of the advantages of teaching, her profession. Keep in mind, Mom has never had her own business, so while she has tons of information and insights, she wouldn't necessarily be my first choice for business advice. Of course, I'm in no way saying that my Mom is a Tormentor! I'm simply stating what I hope is obvious: you must consider the source of any and all advice, business or otherwise. Clearly, Mom wants me to be happy and successful, but she's not going to be my go-to-woman when I get into a business jam or when a tough business decision is needed.

What do you think Mom would say if I were to tell her that I had been struggling financially, and I was about to close a $20,000 deal. I was trying to decide between taking the money, cutting my losses and closing the business or possibly putting the $20,000 back into the business in hopes of bringing in more sales. Which would she recommend?

Mom would say, "Son, take the money and run!"

Now, let's examine Mom's probable answer. What would make her respond that way?

*Lack of business knowledge. She has never owned a business and doesn't understand the level of sacrifice necessary to be successful. She doesn't understand that you must invest in your business.*

*Avoidance of pain. She's also been clear that she wants things easy and simple, and the easiest option that generates the least amount of stress would be to take the money.*

*High level of emotional attachment. I'm her baby, and*

*she can't stand the thought of her baby possibly being stressed out and losing the money. She prefers the avoidance of pressure, even if making a different choice that caused some pressure, could potentially lead to pleasure.*

Now, keep in mind that every situation is different. I'm not saying if you're in a similar situation that Mom's flavor of advice wouldn't be right for you. The point is that you have to understand who's giving the advice before you can really assess whether or not it's good advice.

Rapper KRS-One once said, "If you don't know the history of the author, then you don't know what you have read." The background and belief system of the advisor is important in determining how to interpret what you have read or heard, just as knowing the limits of your advisors helps you to interpret the advice that you get.

In the book, The Cashflow Quadrant, by Robert Kiyosaki, he states that the way in which Baby Boomers, who were raised during the industrial revolution, think is counter-productive to being successful in business. They were taught myths such as:

"Get a good education, so you can get a good job," "Work hard and it'll pay off," "A job offers you security," and "If you want to be rich, save your money."

This mindset is what the educational systems and schools in the United States were founded upon. They don't teach children how to be creative or to be contrapreneurs. They teach them how to be good employees. The corruption and scandals at companies such as Enron illustrate that many of these ideals and beliefs that have been engrained in us since birth are full of fallacies. This consciousness isn't relegated only to Baby Boomers; it's pervasive throughout all generations.

As I look back on all of the formal and informal advisors and mentors from those early days, the truth is that I didn't realize how blessed I was. There was a treasure chest of great support around me. There were people who were giving me advice that could potentially change the way I did business, but honestly, I wasn't ready to take advantage of what was right in front of me.

You're no different. I bet that if I came to your hometown and got to be an invisible visitor who followed you around for one full business day, I'd see you passing up tons of chances to improve your business operations or even the way you think. So, I ask you, "Will you be open to the sound advice of the people who've already walked the halls of business success?"

Take a tip from someone who's not only been there, gotten the t-shirt and even designed the t-shirt: open your heart and mind to the vast mentoring possibilities that are staring you right in the face. Don't be afraid to ask for help. Don't be so proud that you won't stop a bad situation from getting worse. Most of all, tap into the fantastic human resources that are waiting to help you become the best contrapreneur you can become. You'll be glad you did.

# SIX

# Consider The Plan

---

*"As a sponsor of the Houston Black Expo I have had the pleasure of watching this phenomenal event become the largest African American tradeshow in Texas under the dynamic leadership of Jerome Love. Through this event Jerome continues to bring wealth, awareness and a since of wholeness to the community. He is the essence of a* Contrapreneur!*"*

**—Sharon Phillips, First Vice President, Washington Mutual**

I'm not real big on clichés or quotes, but here's one that I've found to be true: "If you fail to plan, you plan to fail."

This adage is so simple that many of us – myself included – miss the impact. It's exactly what Dr. Mason attempted to tell me that day at his house: passion is great, but a plan is supreme.

There is also another "P" that's worth mentioning - pressure.

## THE POWER OF PRESSURE

Pressure can be a good thing. Ask any athlete who's ever performed under extreme situations. It can either bring out the best or the worst in a person. A lot of great things come out of pressure-packed situations. After all, you can't enjoy the sweet taste of a glass of orange juice unless you first apply pressure and squeeze the orange. Pressure, in and of itself, isn't good or bad; it just is. It's what we make of the pressure that provides insights into the kinds of contrapreneurs we become.

We've all heard of stories where a child was trapped under a vehicle, and the mother lifts the car to free the child. Pressure can sometimes actually make you more productive. Sometimes it serves as a way of getting you out of your comfort zone and making you search for more. However, pressure without a plan is a surefire recipe for running a business into the ground and causing yourself a lot of unnecessary frustration.

The fastest way to disaster is to start a business without a plan. You can't just haphazardly jump into something and expect it to work. Sure, sometimes it will work, but continuing to operate in a helter skelter mentality will ultimately mean the demise of your business.

Dr. Mason's words still ring loudly in my ears: "You're operating out of passion, not a plan." I didn't really understand or embrace his words at the time, but they are words that I live by today. You have to have a plan if you want to be successful. Furthermore, a plan takes a lot of the pressure off of you!

When you map out a strategy for where you want to go and how you're going to get there, it gives you confidence. You still have to get the plan "done," but at least you don't have the unnecessary pressure of trying to navigate waters that are completely foreign to you. A roadmap won't guarantee success; it simply makes the journey much smoother.

A good plan should be detailed. The details are what provide the necessary information that will help you to make sound business decisions.

Former U.S. Secretary of State Colin Powell was a dynamic leader, and when asked the key to be a successful leader, noted the importance of a detailed plan. Powell notes in the book, The Leadership Secrets of Colin Powell, by Oren Harari, that the details of the plan change the way in which you look at your options. In addition, he believes, that once you have decided upon a particular option, knowledge of the details will lead to better execution and a leader that has mastered the details of a plan can effectively inspire confidence.

So take a lesson from Colin Powell - creating a plan is imperative in being a successful contrapreneur.

## WHAT IS A PLAN?

"Plan," as defined by Webster's dictionary, is <u>a scheme or method of acting, doing, proceeding, making, etc., developed in advance</u>. I also believe that a plan is the tangible substance of an idea. You have to make your idea into a reality. It has to become something tangible, something that you can refer to or review at a moment's notice. Your plan is what brings your idea to life.

## WHAT IS PASSION?

"Passion" is defined as <u>any powerful or compelling emotion</u>

or feeling. Passion is a feeling, and feelings are based upon emotions. You cannot successfully govern a business with emotions. Emotions have an uncanny way of getting us into undesirable situations. It's like the man who sees his neighbor with a new Mercedes and wants the same level of ego gratification of having a Mercedes, so he buys one too – even though he can't afford it. You know what happens next. He struggles to make his payments. His marriage starts to suffer under the financial strain. He starts to hate his job even more, but he can't leave because he's got that humongous car payment. Do you see what happened here? His emotions promised fulfillment and ego gratification, but in the end his inability to manage his emotions resulted in a higher car note and greater financial frustration.

## PASSION VS. PLAN?

What's the difference between passion and a plan? Ask any married couple to talk about passion versus planning, and most of them will say, "We had incredible passion." You'll never hear, "We had an incredible plan." Most failed marriages all take the same path that leads to the same destination - divorce court. When a married couple first hooks up, they have nothing but glowing remarks to make about each other. He's so cute. She's so fine. We finish each other's sentences. Very few couples ever go to the extent of planning for their marriage. Oh, sure, lots of couples "talk about" their futures, but few of them ever devise a plan for marital success. Can a marriage truly have a greater shot at success with a plan? Of course!

Let's say Scott wants to get married. He wants to maintain his career, have kids, and he desires a mate that can cook and take care of the house. He's looking for a woman who's interested in being a "stay-at-home" mom. That's his plan. Sexist? Maybe, but it's still Scott's plan.

Then there's Sarah. Sarah wants to get married, too. She's in college completing her MBA and has plans to start her own business. She wants a man who is established in the business world – either as an entrepreneur or in a company – who will support her entrepreneurial dreams and aspirations.

Sarah meets Scott, they date for a year, and they are so passionate about one another that they forget all about their individual plans and decide to get married. Well, you already know how this one will probably end up. Divorce. Why? Because they put passion over their respective plans. They were so moved by emotions that they forgot about their plans. If people want to have healthy marriages, they cannot be moved by emotions alone. They must also have a plan.

What does marriage have to do with contrapreneurship? A lot. Business is a lot like marriage. It requires a commitment, love, and passion. It can bring out the best or the worst in you. You'll go through several phases in marriage just as you do in a business. The two are quite synonymous. Like a marriage, passion will only get you so far in business.

For me, this lesson was learned the hard way. Being so passionate about GUGOGS, I disregarded the need for a plan. Passion was going to see me through! It was going to find my customers, pay my office rent, market my business, and find investors. Yep, passion was my salvation, or so I thought. My

I know that the absence of a plan will lead you down a road that's filled with disappointment and despair.

passion blinded me to the point that I thought my logo was the most beautiful logo on the planet. I was already getting ready to meet some of my fashion idols like Armani and Sean "P Diddy" Combs. I was a t-shirt baller in the making. I just knew it.

At the time, the hottest new clothing line on the market was FUBU – For Us By Us. It had been started by four young guys who were not that much older than me. Their line was hip, it was trendy, it was hot, and it was everywhere. If you had any coolness about you, you had some FUBU gear in your closet.

Fueled by scorching passion and a desire to succeed, I set out to make GUGOGS the next big thing. I had dreams of building this fairy tale business that would make me a multi-millionaire many times over. I had dreams of one day being like the FUBU guys; being on various television commercials, in rap videos, and having celebrities sport my apparel. My dreams were to have celebrities walking down the red carpet in a brand new custom suit from the GUGOGS Collection. I had it all mapped out, but I kept hearing Dr. Mason's words ringing in my ear. You've got to have a plan. A business without a plan will eventually end up in destruction.

Destruction is a nice way of describing what happened to my apparel business.

I've learned that some of our greatest disappointments can also become the things that propel us to the next level of greatness. GUGOGS had so much potential, but instead of sitting down and planning the future of the business, I launched an ambitious business with no real focus and no strategy for success. So when I encourage you to make a plan, I speak from experience. I can tell you that the absence of a plan will lead you down a road that's filled with disappointment and despair. You don't want to travel that road. Trust me.

Here are two quick, Planning Points, that'll put you on the fast track to success.

## PLANNING POINT # 1 – SET SOME GOALS

As mentioned earlier, one of the businesses that I currently own is the Texas Black Expo, Inc. This is a non-profit organization that currently organizes and promotes the Houston Black Expo, which is the largest African-American tradeshow in Texas. Organizing a tradeshow of this magnitude affords me the opportunity to meet and learn from hundreds of different business owners and contrapreneurs — from billion dollar companies to start-up businesses.

At our Expo, which is the largest event that my company organizes, we typically have roughly 250 to 300 business vendors. These businesses rent exhibit space at our tradeshow for our two-day festival, which draws more than 20,000 attendees over a two-day period. One of the things that I noticed when speaking with our corporate exhibitors or the large multi-million dollar companies is that they all have very specific goals as it relates to attending the Expo.

Their decision to exhibit with us is not random. They're not simply looking for something to do on the weekend. Some attend with the goal of increasing at retail, while others may want to add 5,000 new names to their database. Others are there to increase their brand's visibility within the African-American community. The goals may vary but the mindset behind all of our corporate exhibitors is the same: successful businesses that know where they are headed have a greater chance at arriving there.

Like our vendors and exhibitors, the Houston Black Expo also has goals for each event. We measure our organizational effectiveness, our sales, and our attendance, among other things. At the close of the Houston Black Expo, we always follow up with our sponsors and exhibitors, and the vast majority are extremely happy with their experience. Their success is a result of developing a plan in advance with measurable goals. They measure their results at the Expo against their initial goal in order to make a determination as to whether or not they were successful. They don't do anything without looking at the overall plan and goal for the company, and this determines the direction of the company.

> If you can't measure your goal there's no way to determine if your business is growing ... It's not just about "what" you're going to accomplish. It's also about "how" you're going to accomplish them.

Prior to our 2005 Expo, I spoke with a well-known billion-dollar insurance company about sponsoring or exhibiting at our event. I shared information on how many people would be there and gave all the exciting testimonials of other sponsors. There was even a small video showing the energy and excitement of the Expo. I gave what was one of my best sales pitches, and they still turned us down.

As a businessman, I know that each time I step up to bat I'm not going to hit a home run. Yet, I was still curious as to why they passed on being a sponsor, so I asked. They told me that their 2005 focus was on national events as opposed to regional ones. Their plans for 2005 had already been put into place when I came calling. They believed that the plan they had in place would help them achieve their overall goals and they had no plans of deviating from their strategy. Although disappointed with the fact that the company was not going to participate in the Expo, you had to respect the fact that they stayed the course and weren't easily distracted from their goals and objectives. It was a good example for me to follow.

In contrast, many small businesses that exhibit at our Expo operate on a fly-by-the-seat-of-their-pants model. Most typically don't have concrete goals in mind. They're looking for exposure and sales. Their success over the weekend is typically determined by those two factors. "Did people see us," and "Did people buy our stuff?" Now, there's nothing wrong with measuring exposure and sales. I just know that there are many other opportunities available beyond those two.

For instance, the networking opportunities over the weekend are staggering. Not only can a company come into contact with consumers and potential customers, but they can also meet potential joint venture partners to build strategic alliances. But first, they have to look beyond the obvious reasons to attend a large tradeshow.

Another company that I own is a real estate company, LHS Realty Group, which specializes in helping homeowners to sell their homes quickly at top dollar. We also deal with a number of investors that are interested in "making money in real estate." Many investors will call and have a sincere desire to prosper or to make money, but they usually don't have any goals in mind. They're just going with the flow. While there's value in flexibility, a plan will help get you to your destination a lot faster than "going with the flow."

Let's stay with the real estate investor for a moment. If you want to be a real estate investor, what is your goal? Are you trying to create cash or cash flow? How much cash or how much cash flow are you trying to create? Let's say your goal is to make $20,000 cash flow per month this year in real estate investing and that you want to buy one house a month. This helps to establish the parameters for each purchase. Armed with that knowledge, we know you will be purchasing only 12 properties and that each must generate more than $1,600 per month to reach your $20,000 cash flow goal.

Depending on your market, whether you're dealing in commercial, multifamily, single family, etc., and the amount of cash you have as an initial investment, this may be a bit unrealistic. At minimum, you'll know what it takes for you to reach your goal. It's that simple. Just by knowing your goals and your parameters and by establishing a plan, you could then narrow down which potential properties to purchase. With this information, you can effectively look at the right properties.

In order for a goal to be effective it must be…

Specific

Realistic

Measurable

## Specific

Specificity is critical to achieving any goal. It's not enough to simply say that we want to produce the country's best Expo; we have to define what that means. It could mean that we want to attract over 50,000 people in three days. It could mean that our goal is to attract top entertainment talent. It could mean that we want a certain number of vendors or exhibitors. In either case, those statements are all specific.

## Realistic

Setting unrealistic goals will only lead to disappointment and a whole lot of heartache. I went to the Magic Show expecting to come back with hundreds of thousands dollars in orders, which was pretty unrealistic for a new clothing line that was exhibiting for the first time. As a result, I went through a lot of unnecessary financial and emotional distress.

Was it realistic for me to say that I wanted 100,000 people to attend the Houston Black Expo in our first year? Probably not. It would have been ambitious given that I didn't know a whole lot about producing large tradeshows. It would have been crazy to think that in the first year I could get all of the top-tier sponsors to believe in our product. Thus, your goal has to be realistic as well.

Contrapreneurs know that goals must be a stretch, but you don't stretch yourself so far that your goals feel unbelievable.

## Measurable

Finally, your goals must be measurable. If you can't measure your goals there's no way to determine if your business is growing. If we go back to some of our small business vendors at the Expo, we'll find that their desire for exposure is a solid objective as long as they are effectively measuring that goal. Many say things like, "I want exposure for my business." That's a great start, but it doesn't break the goal down into clear, concise action steps. Are you going to achieve this exposure by getting 300 business cards dropped in your fish bowl? Are you going to achieve this exposure by having a bright, colorful exhibit space? These are the kinds of questions that every business owner must ask. It's not just about "what" you're going to accomplish. It's also about "how" you're going to accomplish the goals.

## PLANNING POINT #2 – WRITE IT DOWN

What gets written gets our attention. We may not necessarily "do" what gets written, but for me, writing things down helps me to become more productive. Plus, I can always go back and review what I've written down and compare it to where I am and what I am currently doing to determine if I am on course.

The written plan for a business is what is referred to as a business plan. A business plan is critical to the success of any business. It's essential for many reasons but especially if you plan to attract investors or seek any kind of funding for your enterprise. Any prudent bank, investor, or venture capitalist won't even consider funding your business unless you have a written business plan.

This was yet another thing that I learned the hard way. In my decision to take my clothing line national and to exhibit at the Magic Show in Las Vegas, I knew that I needed funding. I'd heard about this thing called a CDC or Community Development Corporation, which specialized in providing money to small business owners with issues that make them less-than-desirable candidates for conventional financing. Issues like; less than perfect credit, bankruptcy or foreclosures.

It was exciting to hear about the program, although I had no clue about how the whole thing worked. I walked into the meeting with my best suit on and listened as they explained their program. As it turns out, the process was fairly simple: give us your business plan, we'll review it, and then we will let you know. This sounded great, except there was just one problem – I didn't have a business plan, and to be honest with you, I had never heard of a business plan! Smiling as if everything was okay, I told them they could expect it by the next week.

Frantically, I left the meeting, immediately whipped out my cell phone, and called my fraternity brother, Alejandro Vasquez, and asked for his help. He then referred me to a book entitled, The Portable MBA in Entrepreneurship by William Bygrave. What a lifesaver! Bygrave's book outlines many useful principles. My favorite was the business plan section, which states that every solid business plan should have these seven key elements:

- Executive Summary

- Company Overview

- Products & Services

- Market Analysis

- Marketing Strategy

- Management Team

- Financials

## EXECUTIVE SUMMARY

The executive summary is arguably the most important part of the business plan. I say this for two primary reasons. First of all, it comes first. It's the first thing that someone will see before they delve into the full business plan. If you start out with what one of my good friends, Jonathan Sprinkles, calls "A Bore and a Snore," anyone reading it will not want more. Be creative. Here's where that passion comes in handy. Channel that passion into the executive summary in a way that makes people want to read more. The best way to think about this section and the entire business plan is this: each sentence sells the next. Never forget that.

The second primary reason to craft a solid executive summary is that its purpose is to capture the heart and essence of your business. A good two-page executive summary will briefly touch on all of the other areas of the business plan. If someone were to read your executive summary, they should go away with a clear understanding of your company.

## COMPANY OVERVIEW

This section of the business plan should go deeper into the story of your company. It should include your mission statement and answer the following: What's your purpose? What's your goal? What do you seek to accomplish? What need are you meeting?

In this section, you should give the history of your company. Who started the company? Where is the company located? When was the company started? Why was the company started? This area should give detailed information on the story of your business. After reading this quick synopsis, the reader should have a good sense of how your business got where it is today.

## PRODUCTS OR SERVICES

What do you do? What do you offer? What business are you in? Even if you don't have a tangible product, you must still be able to convey what business you're in. In other words, let's say you're a training and development company. Your product/service could be the actual seminar. You could also produce educational items such as audio CDs, DVDs, books or curriculums that are used in your seminars.

How much is your product? Where is it available? Most important of all, why would someone want your product? I'm often asked to speak or consult with companies or individuals who are struggling to increase business or sales, and they can't figure out what to do. When speaking with these individuals one of the things that I always focus on is establishing what is called a U.M.P. or Unique Marketing Position. This helps to answer the most important question: Why would someone want your product?

Whatever product or service you offer, you have to understand that consumers have many alternatives, so you must distinguish yourself from your competitors by establishing that

U.M.P. To learn more about establishing a U.M.P. visit www.jeromelove.com.

## MARKET ANALYSIS

The best way to explain this section is in, you guessed it, real estate terms (surprise, surprise)! There are two sides to each real estate transaction. The buyer's agent represents the buyer, and the listing agent represents the seller. I specialize in listing or helping people to sell their homes, so I'm a listing agent.

In my 10 years of business, I have done hundreds of listing presentations, where I present what is known in the industry as a CMA. CMA stands for Comparative Market Analysis. The key to selling a home is to have it priced properly. The value of the subject property has very little to do with that actual property. It has more to do with all of the other homes in the area. Inherently, every seller wants me to add to the suggested value of their home because they have hardwood floors or some other feature that they believe is the best thing since ice cream. It's my job to explain to them that in order to properly value their home, they must compare their home to others that have sold in the market and then price theirs accordingly.

A CMA illustrates to the seller what other homes are selling for, thereby giving the seller clues about how their home should be priced.

It's the same in business, unless you're an island where you have a monopoly in a certain industry or field. In order to be successful, you must consider your market. The market includes your competitors as well as your customers. Customers can also be referred to as your demographic. If you sell high-priced art, you probably don't want to open a store in a low-income neighborhood. Why? Because those people aren't your target demographic! You wouldn't put dog food in a fish tank, would you? Of course not!

You must also be aware of your competitors. It's important to be objective. Never think that your product is so great that no one can touch you. That's the kiss of death!

In order to keep your head above water during those lean years of launching your business you need cash reserves or some kind of personal savings.

I thought GUGOGS was so phenomenal that I didn't need a plan. In my mind there was no need to think about competitors. Boy was I wrong!

The market analysis is where you demonstrate your knowledge and expertise in a certain area or field. It also will illustrate to customers or clients that you're the expert on your product or service.

## MARKETING STRATEGY

This is one of my favorite topics. I love marketing. Always keep in mind that no matter what type of business that you have, it's nothing without customers. This is where you map out your plan for reaching the market outlined in the previous section. How will you spread your message? Will it be on TV, Radio, Direct Mail, Billboards or the Internet? Will you market your business using a diverse marketing mix?

In this area, you should be very specific, including when the advertising will start. How often will you advertise? How long will you advertise? With a bit of research, you can market your business without breaking the bank. Again, a solid plan will help you maximize your marketing dollars.

## MANAGEMENT TEAM

The management team section should be the easiest section to write. This is your time to shine. In this section, you should include information on your credentials. Who are you? How did you get to where you are today? What degrees do you have? What awards or other recognitions have you received? You will also need to discuss your role with the company. Go through this same process for any key individuals on your company's management team roster.

## FINANCIALS

This is arguably the second most important part of your business plan. If you're seeking investors, it's number one. Why? Because the numbers don't lie. They give the true picture or story of your company, and in reality, they are the true benchmarks of a successful business.

Essentially, your financials are equivalent to your scorecard. At minimum, this section should include these two financial statements – an income statement and a balance sheet.

## INCOME STATEMENT

An income statement is also referred to as a Profit and Loss statement or P&L statement. It summarizes your company's financial operations for a specific period of time. It should show the net profit or loss for the period by showing the company's revenues and expenses.

## BALANCE SHEET

The Balance Sheet shows the financial position of a business at a particular point in time or on a particular day. Sometimes it's referred to as the Statement of Financial Position, or Statement of Financial Condition. It will include three primary categories: assets, liabilities and owner's equity.

In my GUGOGS executive summary and overview, I could truthfully say "I exhibited my line of clothing at one of the largest apparel trade shows in the world. In addition, I have stores carrying my products in Illinois, Ohio and Michigan. The United States Marine Corps picked up my full women's line." That sounds pretty exciting. It sounds like GUGOGS is doing well financially, right? Now let's look at some actual numbers on

Exhibit A and then show how they would be illustrated in financial statements.

Words can sometimes be misleading, but numbers don't lie. Listening to the words in the executive summary may have given the impression that we were financially stable and sound, but when you take a look at the financial statement you get the real story. We had lost $11,950 and was more than $20,000 in debt.

One final note: This income statement is done on an accrual basis. What this means is that the income is recorded when it is earned, not when the cash is received. Although the sales that I had were being paid on a net 30 (e.g. 30 days after product is delivered), they show as income during this period.

## Cash Flow Statement

Another commonly used statement that I suggest you include in your business plan is the Cash Flow Statement. This statement is almost identical to the income statement except that it is more detailed. It records the receipts and expenditures during a specific period. Remember, the income statement shows total income and expenses over a time period. The Cash Flow Statement will

# EXHIBIT A

## INCOME / REVENUE

| Buyer | No. Bought | Sale Amount$15 | Terms |
|---|---|---|---|
| Ohio store: | 40 shirts | $600 | Net 30 |
| Illinois store: | 30 shirts | $450 | Net 30 |
| Michigan store: | 60 shirts | $900 | Net 30 |
| U.S. Marines | 70 shirts | $1,050 | Net 60 |
| Total Sales = | | $3,000 | |

## EXPENSES

| Expense | Total |
|---|---|
| Booth Rental | $6,000 |
| Airline Tickets | $1,800 |
| Display Items | $1,500 |
| Freight Charges | $900 |
| Flyers | $800 |
| Inventory | $3,000 |
| Meals | $300 |
| Hotel | $650 |
| Display Design | $3,000 |
| Total Expense = | $17,950 |

## LOANS / DEBT

| | |
|---|---|
| CDC Loan | $20,000 |
| Credit Card Debt | $2,500 |
| Total Debt = | $22,500 |

# GUGOGS APPAREL
# INCOME STATEMENT

From November 1, 1999 to March 1, 2000

## REVENUE

| | |
|---|---|
| Shirt Sales | $3,000 |
| Total Income | $3,000 |

## EXPENSES

| | |
|---|---|
| Airfare | $1,800 |
| Booth Rental | $6,000 |
| Display Items | $1,500 |
| Freight Charges | $900 |
| Flyers | $800 |
| Inventory | $3,000 |
| Meals | $300 |
| Hotel | $650 |
| Display Design | $3,000 |
| Total Expenses | $17,950 |
| **Net Income** | **($14,950)** |

# GUGOGS APPAREL
# BALANCE SHEET

As of March 1, 2000

## ASSETS

| | |
|---|---|
| Cash | $4,550 |
| Accounts Receivable | $3,000 |
| Inventory | $3,000 |
| Total Assets | $10,550 |

## LIABILITIES

| | |
|---|---|
| Short Term Debt (Credit Card) | $2,500 |
| Long Term Debt (CDC Loan) | $20,000 |
| Total Liabilities | $22,500 |

## EQUITY

| | |
|---|---|
| Owner's Equity | -$11,950 |
| Total Equity | -$11,950 |
| Total Liabilities & Owners Equity | $10,550 |

record or show when a transaction occurred. I typically use a monthly Cash Flow Statement, but you can break it down by weeks or even by day if you like.

Clearly, I only touched on the business plan. It is critical to your success and should be taken very seriously. For more information, I strongly suggest that you read the book, The Portable MBA in Entrepreneurship.

Another invaluable resource is an organization called S.C.O.R.E. The acronym stands for the Senior Corps of Retired Executives. These are retired former CEO's, businessmen, and presidents of major companies who dedicate their time to counseling businessmen and women. Best of all, it's free! To find your local S.C.O.R.E. office, visit www.score.org.

# SEVEN

# Consider Your Finances

---

*"What Jerome has accomplished is simply phenomenal. Get Up, Get Out, Get Something isn't just a catchy title, it's an empowering message that defines Jerome's life and should be required reading for students everywhere!"*

**—Brenda Burt, Director, Multicultural Information Center**

**The University of Texas at Austin**

Research shows that more than 70 percent of all start-up companies will fail within the first year. Of the remaining 30 percent, less than half will make it past year two. Research also shows that one of the primary reasons for the lack of success in new businesses is undercapitalization – not enough money. So my question to you is: What is your financial plan for the future? How will you finance your business venture? How will you make it when you can't pay yourself? These are not rhetorical questions. They are real questions that every contrapreneur must answer.

Outside of GUGOGS, my first business endeavor was in the real estate business as an agent. As a realtor, you are an independent contractor whose license is held with a broker. It's kind of like having a franchise, as you have the benefits of using the name of your broker, which in many cases is more recognized and reputable. The downside is that you don't draw a salary. During my junior year in college, I earned my real estate license and began to work as an apartment locator. The money was pretty good, and it was a perfect summer job. At the time, the University of Texas at Austin was among the largest universities in the country, and the vast majority of their 50,000-plus students moved during the summer months. As a result of this trend, 85 percent of my income came during June, July, and August.

Upon graduating from college and getting into debt with GUGOGS, I needed a more consistent income. So the search began for a new broker, as I desired to go into full time real estate sales.

In May 2000, I began my full-time real estate career with a local Prudential franchise. I was eager to start my new career, as were many of the nine other new agents that began training with me. After only two months of training, only four of the original nine new agents were still with the company. Within six months, that number dropped to two. I was one of the two. It is my belief that the other seven simply were not prepared for what the job required.

Research shows that it will take a new real estate agent on average six months to make his first sale. That's a full six months with no income, yet all the same expenses. As Denzel Washington jokingly said in an interview when asked about why he works so hard, "Because Mr. Bill-man do be coming." Yes, "do be coming"! Get over the grammar, you get the point. Most of the agents that started with me had the potential to succeed, but because they weren't prepared, they couldn't hang. I was motivated to keep working, because I had to cover my expenses and keep food on the table. Dreaming will only get you so far, because in the end, dreams don't keep the electricity on!

Now as a broker, I see this phenomenon over and over again.

You get agents who are excited about "making money in real estate;" agents who are gung ho about starting with your company. Two to three months down the line, the excitement begins to dissipate as the bills begin to mount, and suddenly, the agents realize that making money in real estate is hard work! Then, they start working a part-time job, and pretty soon real estate falls by the wayside, as their part-time becomes full-time.

All of these agents had potential, but the odds were overwhelmingly stacked against them, just as they are against any new business owner. You have to know that when you start a business, unless you have a rich uncle, or just a pot load of money, there will most likely be a period of famine. In order to survive the famine, you must have a plan in place to give your business the best possible chance at success.

## MASTER YOUR SAVING PLAN

In order to keep your head above water during those lean years of launching your business, you need cash reserves or some kind of personal savings.

To determine how much you will need to save, my suggestion

is that you first calculate your minimum monthly living expenses. Minimum monthly living expenses, in my definition, are the bare essentials necessary to survive. For me, this would be items such as groceries, mortgage or rent, gas, utilities (electric, gas, water), insurance, phone, and car payment. That's it, just the bare essentials. No dining out, pack a lunch. No movies - get used to TNT or Lifetime, and guys, no video games!

After you tally your minimum expenses, multiply that number by a minimum of six, and now you have your savings goal. For instance, if your total is $2,000, then your goal is $12,000. Ideally, I would suggest that you have at least a nine-month reserve, but you'll need to decide what is best for your situation.

In order to reach this goal, take a look at your current monthly expenses. Anything that doesn't fall into the category of bare essentials, get rid of it! Whatever the amount that you find you have been spending on non-essential items, put it towards savings. So say for example you go to dinner and a movie twice a week, which costs $50 a week, or $200 dollars a month, you also shop at least once a month, which costs $150, and lastly, you eat out on your lunch break at least three times a week, costing you $40 a week or $160 a month. You tally those unnecessary expenses, and the total is $510. Now you have $510 dollars a month going toward your saving!

Now I know what you are probably thinking: "If my savings goal is $12,000, it will take almost two years. That's too long!"

Let me ask you this question: Would you rather spend two years saving in order to have a successful business that lasts a lifetime, or would you rather start a business now, prematurely, and fail? I guarantee you that two years is nothing compared to five, ten, maybe even fifteen years of frustration in having to work a job in order to pay back debt from a failed business. Trust me, I know!

Unfortunately, our culture has taught us to believe in immediate gratification. Thus, the status quo is to get whatever you want now, be in debt, and die broke.

Contrapreneurs oppose the status quo and understand the importance of patience and the value of delayed gratification.

Keep in mind that I do understand that everyone's situation is different. You may have additional bare essentials, such as medications or daycare, but understand that in starting a business, you will probably experience some lean times, so you must learn to live conservatively.

## MAINTAIN FOCUS

Of all my closest college friends, I'm the only one who is a full-time business owner. Upon graduating from college, most of my friends went into corporate America. They were making decent money and living the good life. At holiday gatherings, most of them would drive up in their Expeditions, Range Rovers, or other luxury vehicles. I was still driving my same little Nissan from college. They were dressed in the latest designer threads from Armani, and I was rocking Levis. We seemed to be in two different worlds, and to be honest, I envied their "success." But I told myself that one day I would be able to afford everything they had and more. It was all about staying the course and not losing focus.

The only thing that helped me during those times was my commitment to maintain my focus on my ultimate goal and vision. I understood where I was going, and knew what needed to be done to get there. I told myself that I could wait on all of the "trappings of success." When fitted for my first custom suit, I recall thinking about those times and it made me appreciate my success even more.

Although I glamorized the lives of many of my college buddies, the reality is that the prosperous lifestyles that they appeared to be living were really a façade. They only thought they had job security. As an employee, they were only one pink slip away from the poor house. One downsizing away from the welfare line. By working in corporate America, they were putting their family's financial well being in the hands of someone else, their company's CEO or leadership. They were living in a bubble. A bubble that could burst at any moment. They had a false sense of security. When thinking about it, I was the fortunate one. At least as a businessman I was guiding my own ship!

As a business owner, you have chosen to control your own destiny. You're not depending on someone else to create the life you want and deserve. I applaud you for that. As you continue to forge ahead toward record-breaking business success, remember this - there are two places to sign a check – on the front and on the back. My decision, a long time ago, was to be the one who gets to sign in that special place on the front, and I encourage you to do the same.

## MANAGE YOUR CREDIT

Most of my college buddies have a lot of nice things, expensive cars and big houses, but with that almost always comes a ton of debt. As a result of the debt that they have accumulated, unless they are being intentional about saving and investing their money, they are now caught in the trap of corporate America.

Being a new business owner, you can't afford to try to keep up with the Joneses. The Joneses are probably so debt-ridden and caught up in their extravagant lifestyle that they don't realize how close they are to destruction. I know individuals today who had all the nice items listed above and were laid off. Now the items that they once called a blessing, are now a curse, because they got them before they could afford them. That is the essence of credit. Credit is a tool that allows you to have stuff before you can afford it.

Many of you reading this may think that I'm a pretty cheap and miserly fellow, right? I'm not. I like nice things, and one day,

I will drive the overpriced luxury vehicle and live in the big house on the lake. These are luxuries, and my belief is that luxuries are to be earned. They are the results of success — not the symbols of success. If you reward yourself before you've earned it, you'll not only jeopardize your emotional and mental health, but also the health and well being of your business. In the word of financial guru and author Dave Ramsey, "Live like no one else today, so you can live like no one else tomorrow."

When starting the Houston Black Expo, I was living in a 30-year-old house with two roommates. Yep, the president of the largest African-American tradeshow in Texas was living in a 1600 square foot house in an area that most wouldn't classify as nice - with two roommates! I remember rubbing elbows with many of the most prosperous business leaders in Houston, riding in their BMW's, and attending events at their mini-mansions overlooking the lake. It was hard being exposed to a life that, on many levels I wanted but couldn't have at the moment. Sure, I could have upgraded my car and even moved into a nicer house, but at what expense? I wasn't willing to risk losing my long-term success for short-term gratification. It was tempting, but my conviction was that if I rewarded myself prematurely, my business would be jeopardized, so I chose to wait.

Be patient. Protect and manage your credit wisely. Credit cards are not evil; they're a great tool when properly used. If you're one of those people who find it hard to discipline yourself after watching an episode of "MTV Cribs" or "Lifestyles of The Rich & Famous," then cut up your credit cards right now! You will thank me later.

## MEET A BANKER

Any healthy business will begin to grow, and with that growth, more resources will be needed. At some point you may even need to take out a loan from a bank. This may sound a bit oxymoronic coming after my last point advising you not to incur any debt, but it's not. For me, there are two types of debt: consumption debt and investment debt.

## CONSUMPTION DEBT

Consumption debt is debt that is incurred to consume. All of the stuff listed above is consumption debt, and yes, even your home is consumption. Consumption debt is any type of debt that is incurred that only takes money out of your pocket but rarely, if ever, puts money in your pocket.

## INVESTMENT DEBT

Investment debt is necessary debt that is incurred to make you money. It is debt that is intended to put money in your pocket. The loan taken from the CDC would be an example of investment debt. I got the loan to do a tradeshow that I thought would put money in my pocket. I use this example, because that, in fact, did not happen: it took money out of my pocket. However this was not the intent.

Knowing that you may one day need funding for your business, I'd strongly admonish you to begin to establish a relationship with a banker. No one likes a person who only comes around when they need something. Meet your banker today when you don't need anything to make preparations for the day that you do. You will still need to have your financials in order, maintain your credit, and have all your other ducks in a row, but it always helps if you have someone there on the bank's side who is in your corner.

## FINANCING YOUR BUSINESS

You've got the idea, you've got the passion, and now you've got the plan, but as the old Wendy's hamburger advertisements used to say, "Where's the beef?" Where are you going to get the money to start the business?

There are many, many ways to fund your business. Here are three traditional sources.

- Bank Loans
- Venture Capital
- Angel Investor

### BANK LOAN

It has been my experience that the top priority of a bank is to make sure that you have the capacity to repay the loan. In order to receive a loan from a bank, they will look for what is sometimes referred to as the Three C's: Credit, Collateral, and Cash Flow. Some bankers include two additional C's: Character and Capital. We will just focus on the others, as, in my opinion, they are the most important.

### *Credit*

Your credit score is simply an indicator of your credit worthiness. The scores range from 350 to 850, with 850 being perfect in a lender's mind. It shows your prior credit history and provides insight (allegedly) into your character. If you have a history of not paying your bills or paying your bills late, most bankers will assume that you lack financial integrity. As a result, they will most likely deny your loan request unless you are extremely strong in the other two C's. Make sure you plan for your future today by living within your means and not overextending your credit, as it can have severe repercussions in the future.

### *Collateral*

Collateral is an asset that secures a loan. For instance, if you own real estate, boats or cars, the bank may ask that you put those assets up as collateral. In the event that you default on your loan, they can take your assets to recoup some of their costs.

### *Cash Flow*

The last C is cash flow. In simple terms, cash flow is exactly as it sounds: how cash flows through your business. It gives the bank an idea of your capacity to repay the loan. This is where your financial statements will come in handy. In order to verify your financial information, they will typically request a minimum of two years of tax returns. This will be difficult to illustrate if you are a start-up business.

Again, a bank's primary concern is ensuring that you have the capacity to repay the loan. Therefore, they are mostly interested in your history, which they feel will help to predict the future, and quite frankly, their ability to get their money back. For a typical banker, your overall business plan carries less weight than your credit and financial picture.

One advantage to securing a bank loan is that you maintain control of your business. There is minimal risk and minimal cost to you. Additionally, no matter how much money you make or how successful you become, you pay the same amount each month to the bank. The drawbacks are that you're stuck with a monthly payment that is not contingent upon the business' success or failure. In the unfortunate instance that you default on your payment, your credit will be jeopardized, and you run the risk of losing any assets that you may have pledged as collateral.

## VENTURE CAPITAL

Venture capital, is defined by the American Heritage Dictionary as money made available for investment in innovative enterprises or research, in which both the risk of loss and the potential for profit may be considerable.

In essence, venture capital is money given by an organization or individual that is looking for a big return. In my opinion, the primary concern of a venture capitalist isn't your ability to repay the money, but your ability to tremendously grow the businesses profits so that they can share in the profits.

The major advantage to venture capital is that if the business should fail, typically there are little or no repercussions. These people knew the risks going into the deal. The next primary benefit is that if you're lacking in any of the areas that the bank requires, a venture capitalist really doesn't care. Let me restate that to say, the V.C. may care, but may be willing to look past the issues if you have a solid concept or idea. A business plan is going to mean more to these people, as it will show your plan for growth and their chances of making a lot of money.

The vast majority of people that go to venture capitalists are people that can't get funding from traditional sources. Venture capitalists are not necessarily turned off by businessmen with credit issues. They're not likely to judge a new or unproven business. In addition to these advantages, you don't have a monthly payment hanging over your head, so you can focus on growing your business.

The big drawback to venture capital funding, depending on how the deal is structured, is that you typically lose control of the business. A venture capitalist will typically want the majority share of your company and/or a guaranteed return on investment. On top of that, they get their cut first as the business makes money. If a venture capitalist has a major stake in your company, they will also typically want to be in on the decision-making process and be updated on what's happening with the business. The good part of this is that by being vested, they most likely will work with you to build the business, bringing invaluable resources to the table such as: intellectual capital, new networks of people, and necessary office supplies and equipment. A bank could care less about who's running your business, just as long as the note is paid. In the long run, you'll pay a higher premium by going the V.C. route but if you're starting a business that has the potential of say, Yahoo or Google, venture capital may be the way to go.

## ANGEL INVESTOR

In my opinion, the absolute best option when seeking funding for your business is an angel investor. This is someone who believes in what you are doing, believes in you, and gives you the money you need for business with little or no strings attached. This could be your mom, dad, family friend, or anyone in-between.

The benefits of angel investors are obvious. You don't have to jump through all of the hoops inherent in conventional bank loans or venture capital. Angel investors make investments based on your relationship. This doesn't mean that the Angel will not want to see a business plan, so be sure you come prepared to reveal your plans for the enterprise just as you would if you were meeting with a banker. The major drawback would be the potential damage done to the relationship if the business fails or if there's an expectation of repayment of the money.

The best way to combat this potential drawback is to draft an agreement stating all the "deal points" so that everyone is clear from the start. Of course, even the best intentions sometimes aren't able to stop a relationship from turning sour. My advice is to get it in writing, communicate openly and pray for a miracle. Guess what? You just might get one!

# EIGHT

# Confirm Your Assets

---

*"Jerome successfully integrates practical business concepts with sound business principles, resulting in his out-of-the-box, against the grain, non-traditional, and highly original invention of Contrapreneurship! Best of all, it's more than just theory, because he inspires the reader along the way with a real-life testimonial of how he employed the principle to build the largest tradeshow of its kind in the southern U.S. in only three short years... unheard of!"*

**—Shannon Cormier, Ph.D., Business Incubation Expert**

My motto is simple: you've got to use what you've got to get what you want.

The Houston Black Expo was started by chance. I saw a tremendous void within Houston's business community and wanted to fill it. The only problem was that I didn't know squat about the tradeshow business. I didn't have any local connections to speak of and didn't have the seed money to start the enterprise. That didn't stop me from going after what I wanted. I was determined to start this business, no matter what it took. Though it was not evident, there was a great deal going for me — there were lots of assets, if you will.

The GUGOGS fiasco left me with a mountain of debt. That's part of the reason real estate became my full time career. It gave me enough income to pay my bills while moonlighting on the side with the tradeshow business.

The last tradeshow at which I exhibited under the GUGOGS brand was the Dallas Black Expo. It was surprising to me that in a city the size of Dallas, at the time, it was their first annual event.

This was June of 2002, right around the time I had decided to move to the Houston area. I did a little sniffing around and discovered that like Dallas, Houston didn't currently have a black expo. After talking to a number of people who'd lived in Houston or in the area for a while, I learned that Houston hadn't had a large African-American tradeshow in years. I was excited by the possibilities and anxious all at the same time.

A month passed, and all of that excitement hadn't led me to anything beyond my Expo idea. Then one night it happened. I was awakened by what was either a dream or a vision, I'm still not clear. In my vision there were thousands of people attending this event, hundreds of businesses and unlimited possibilities of helping others grow and develop their businesses. I saw an

> I personally believe we all need God yet the world has tried to get us to believe that if we have the right clothes, drive the right car or have the right amount of money in the bank that we somehow escape some of life's challenges. Not necessarily so.

incredible opportunity to build a dynamic marketing machine that could help to build and perpetuate my own businesses. This experience propelled me to move forward with the idea.

There was just one problem: I had no money to invest in my dream. Although I was living comfortably, most of my assets were tied up in real estate, and to be honest, my actual asset total was far less than the $200,000 needed to make this event happen.

I was in a real dilemma. Should I take out a loan as I had

done with GUGOGS? I was a bit leery of going down that path again. Thus, I began to think and pray about finding a partner or investor to help me make the Houston Black Expo a reality.

Somewhere around this time my pastor preached a message that changed my life. One of his points was that as a Christian, you have to understand that everyone needs God whether they know it or not. He then began to talk about how we sometimes feel more comfortable trying to tell people who we feel are beneath us about God. People like the homeless or drug addicts. We believe those people need God, not us.

For instance, let's say you run into Oprah at the mall. You'd be less likely to share your faith with her than you would someone who's down on his luck. He went on to say that we somehow think Oprah doesn't need God because she has money. I personally believe that we all need God, yet the world has tried to get us to believe that if we have the right clothes, drive the right car or have the right amount of money in the bank, we somehow escape some of life's challenges. Not necessarily so. Money is great. It gives people the freedom to lead amazing lives and to be of great service to the world, but a life without spiritual connection isn't much of a life. My relationship with God is one of my greatest assets.

Soon after hearing my pastor's sermon I went to lunch with a wealthy friend - a friend who had, on many occasions, expressed an anti-Christian worldview. He was an agnostic – someone who believes it is not possible to have absolute or certain knowledge of God. Given his perspective on God and his financial status, I never really thought much about sharing my faith with him, but after hearing my pastor's message I was compelled to step up to the plate and broach the conversation about my beliefs.

The next time we went to lunch, I made it a point to share my faith in an attempt to help him get a better understanding of God. We had a great time and a spirited conversation. I learned a lot about him and he learned a lot about me. He left lunch still believing as he had before, but I believe our conversation gave him a higher respect for me.

Now what does this story have to do with getting seed money for your business? And what does it have to do with confirming your assets?

Well, the next time we had lunch, he told me that he was looking to invest some money into some business ventures and that if I had any deals working, and needed money, he'd supply the cash if I did the legwork. I couldn't believe my ears. That lunch led to my friend lending me the money to launch the Houston Black Expo. There was no contract and no promissory note. He simply invested in the company because he believed in me. Of course, his investment gave him part ownership in the company at the time, but essentially, he made his decision based on his belief in my ability to turn the Expo into a successful business. That was one of the best lunches of my life!

Obstacle Number One was out of the way. It was on to the next two.

The next challenge was experience. I had none. Not when it came to running a tradeshow business. Nor did I have experience in securing corporate sponsorships. This obstacle made the first one pale by comparison. Still, I was ready. After all, I did know something about tradeshows. I'd been an exhibitor or vendor at nearly 20 different shows. How hard could it be? I was about to find out.

In December of 2002, I formed Texas Black Expo, Inc. I immediately went to other tradeshows and Black Expo websites and began to model our marketing based on what was on theirs. I developed our sponsor packet, vendor packet and website. I even designed business cards, a logo, folders, and envelopes that reflected my vision. I was the salesperson, business development director and head bottle washer for the company. I was doing it all.

At the time, Austin, TX was still my home, so I began scheduling meetings and appointments with people in Houston while driving back and forth from Austin to Houston, which is about 156 miles one way. This trip was made from January to August 2003. The first show was scheduled for May of 2004.

Meetings and phone calls became tedious. Many times, I felt I was getting the run-around. I'd call an executive in the Marketing Department, who would say, talk to the Community Relations Manager. I'd call the Community Relations Manager, and he would say talk to our Community Liaison. It just kept going back and forth. Then, when I'd actually get to the right person they'd say, "Call me in October. That's when our calendar year begins" or "Call me after the first of the year." I felt I was getting nowhere. I needed to confirm my assets - to confirm all of the things that were working for me. As you may know, it's hard to do that when nothing appears to be going your way!

Then one day there was a breakthrough. After courting this one company, they verbally committed to title sponsorship. They told me to send the contract, and they would get it signed immediately and get it back to me. I drafted the agreement, sent it over, and then waited on an executed agreement for a month or so. The wait was excruciating. I couldn't take it, so I decided to call to check the status. That's when I was told that a more senior executive vetoed the decision.

That was in July 2003, so although I was very disappointed, I wasn't broken. There was almost a whole year to get another title sponsor. I also submitted a proposal to HEB, a Texas-based grocery store chain that I thought would be a perfect title sponsor. They turned me down, too, but I kept fighting.

Another visit to the Dallas Black Expo proved fruitful. I met a gentleman there who worked with an Ohio-based food company. We discussed the Houston Black Expo, and he gave me his opinion on some of the concerns of the Texas-based grocery store chain that had turned me down. He shared with me some of the concerns that his company had with the Houston market, then he gave me another grocery store contact – ironically, at HEB. I reached out to this new contact and went through several rounds of being passed around within the company.

In my mind, I was just being blown off, and it was looking pretty dim. Then in September of 2003, HEB hired James Harris, as the new representative in their marketing department. He was from Indianapolis, Indiana and very familiar with the success of the Indiana Black Expo. He understood the potential for his company, and most importantly, he saw the opportunity staring him straight in the face with the Houston Black Expo.

> Write down or verbally remind yourself that you've got it going on in more areas than you realize.

In February of 2004, HEB officially became our title sponsor. Didn't I tell you that if you expect a miracle, you just might get one?

Before landing my first big sponsor, I was still unsure how the event would happen. The final hurdle to clear was my inexperience. I fumbled along, trying different things to promote and make the Expo happen, but the truth is that I had no idea what to do. That's when another angel landed on my doorstep.

I received a call in September of 2003 from a gentleman from Atlanta. When he gave me his name, it sounded familiar, but I couldn't quite figure out how I knew him. It turned out that this gentleman was the former Marketing Director of Black Expo USA, which, at one time, did Black Expos in 17 different cities. This guy was big time. He was also the show director for the Atlanta Black Expo, where I'd exhibited two years prior.

As we continued to talk, he told me that he had left Atlanta and was now in Houston and he wanted to help me put together the show. He sat down and counseled me on how to put everything together. He was a godsend. Now with this new support, everything was falling into place.

On May 15, 2004, the Houston Black Expo had its official opening and ribbon cutting ceremony in Hall C at the Reliant Center. It was a grand event with major celebrities, more than

8,000 people, 200-plus businesses and plenty of fanfare. We even had the support and attendance of the Mayor of Houston, who offered some inspiring remarks. For me, that was one of the greatest experiences of my life. Having an idea or a dream and seeing that dream or vision manifest itself was so surreal.

There were many things that made that day special for me: the attendance, the energy and the networking of businesses, and consumers from all over the city. But the cherry on the sundae was that my team and I had built the largest African-American tradeshow in the state of Texas on a wing and a little prayer. Okay, a lot of prayer.

If you take anything from my tradeshow journey, hopefully it's that you can accomplish anything you want if you just confirm your assets, believe in those strengths, and take action in the direction of your goals. I had no idea how the Expo was going to happen. I just started crawling, then walking, and finally, believing that it was going to happen. As the saying goes, "You can't walk on water unless you first get out of the boat!"

You've heard it a million times, but nonetheless, it's true. You were born with everything that you need to be a success.

Everything! Even if you can't see it right now, it's still there. There are people who are waiting for you to ask them to invest in your dreams. People who are looking for partners to do exactly what you're doing. Collaboration can be a beautiful thing. First, you have to confirm what you have, and believe me, you've got a lot going for you.

Once you know what you have, it's a lot easier to fill in the missing pieces. There are no excuses for not living a charmed life and building a successful business. I'm a living witness that it can be done. So what are you waiting on? It's time to go for it!

However, before you go for it, do one thing right now. Confirm those assets! Write down or verbally remind yourself that you've got it going on in more areas than you realize. Go ahead, confirm your strengths, and most of all, be yourself. That's an asset in and of itself. Don't believe me? Then keep reading!

Some of you may remember the late Steve Irwin. Irwin was a quirky, somewhat weird, animal lover. When Irwin hit the scene, many within his native country of Australia hated him and viewed him as an embarrassment to their country. Americans were the first to embrace and love his zeal for animals and his somewhat quirky behavior. Steve Irwin was just being Steve Irwin. He would talk about his adventures and animals like they were the most fascinating things on the planet! Irwin was doing what he loved, and he was succeeding because he knew that his biggest asset was in just being himself. When he went on the air, he'd become all animated and excited. Each time he stepped into a new adventure, he was confirming his assets; his own strengths. His passion for life showed and eventually made him an international television star. His show, "The Crocodile Hunter," became a smash hit, was syndicated globally, and made Irwin a household name.

That's why even in writing this book, I choose to express myself. It is written "my way." You may notice a bit of slang, and some of my grammar is sure to drive your typical English teacher crazy. But, as a contrapreneur, you have to be willing to step out and do things differently!

Imagine if Irwin had tried to fit in with the crowd, or to alter his behavior to please others. He would have lost his value and probably wouldn't have experienced much success.

The lesson is clear: be yourself.

# NINE

# Content of Your Character

---

*"Contrapreneurship is an easy to read guide to building a successful business that I'd recommend to anyone. It's filled with practical advice and strategies that will help any business large or small go to the next level. It has challenged me to think outside the box."*

**—Francis Page, Jr., Publisher, Houston Style Magazine**

Dr. Martin Luther King, Jr., in his famous "I Have A Dream" speech, said that he dreamed of a day when his children would not be judged by the color of their skin but by the content of their character.

In business, people will often buy the person long before they buy the product. Thus, you must consider how your customers and potential customers view your character.

Character can be defined as your moral or ethical quality. People should not have to guess with you or try to figure out which angle you are coming from. They have to know that you are reliable and dependable. They also need to know that you are fair and would not take advantage of them just to make a quick buck. I once heard someone describe a well-known billionaire as being a "mean, cut-throat SOB". He then went on to say, "I ain't mad at him, that's why he's a billionaire and I'm not."

Jack Welch, former Chairman and CEO of General Electric was a phenomenal leader. General Electric's value, during the 20 years that Welch was its leader, increased from $13 billion to more than $100 billion. From 1981 to 2001, General Electric was revered as one of America's most successful and well-known companies and the leadership and management of Welch became almost legendary. His management style and leadership skills are still to this day, both admired and imitated by business leaders worldwide.

Welch, was a tremendous leader, who believed in honesty and integrity. In the book Jack Welch Speaks by Janet Lowe, he was quoted as saying "You should always tell the truth, because they know the truth anyway." Welch believes in honesty and feels that is the key to success in business. He believed that, "Excellence & Competitiveness are totally compatible with honesty and integrity. The A student, the four-minute miler, the high-jump record holder, all strong winners can achieve those results without resorting to cheating. People who cheat are simply weak."

Contrapreneurs are not weak. Contrapreneurs operate with integrity.

Unfortunately, many businessmen and women would do anything to make a buck. If that means stepping over someone else, they'll do it. True contrapreneurs don't operate this way. They understand the laws of reciprocity – that what goes around comes around. Sure, you may be able to make quick money now, but what about your future? What about having a conscience and being able to sleep at night knowing that you've done the right thing?

I believe that character is who you are when nobody but God is watching.

# TEN

# Concentrate On the Positive

---

*"The principles & insights in* Contrapreneurship *are presented in a simplistic manner that I thoroughly enjoyed. It is an inspiring, empowering, & practical book that I wish I would have had 10 year ago when I started in business!"*

**—Keith J Davis Sr., Publisher D-Mars Business Journal,**

**President & CEO of D-Mars.com**

Starting my own business was one of the most exhilarating experiences of my life. Since you are reading this book, I assume you know exactly what I'm talking about. Yet, while it's been an amazing ride, it hasn't been without its challenges. One of the principles that has helped me keep my eyes on the prize has been my commitment to concentrate on the positive.

There were days and nights when I'd look at myself and say, "What are you doing?"

Most nights I couldn't answer that question, but I stayed in the fight, because I knew there was more to my life than that $420 a week job I once had.

As a business owner, you have to be a thermostat and not a thermometer. A thermometer adjusts to the climate of the environment, while a thermostat sets the climate of the environment. Powerful difference, isn't it? When you own a business or you're trying to start a business, there will be tons of negative situations that will attempt to adjust your emotional climate and make you negative. However, you must learn how to set your own emotional climate and not focus on all of the negative things around you. You'll be surprised to find out how much more productive you'll become if you remain positive. You'll also be surprised to find out how your new outlook will influence the attitudes and perceptions of those around you.

> ... always remember that perception is greater than reality.

In the book, Trump 101: The Way to Success, billionaire businessman Donald Trump states, "Persistence is essential because you can't just start out being positive and then throw in the towel at the first sign of trouble. You have to stay positive because success rarely occurs overnight."

Trump discusses very candidly many of his concerns and fears when doing the show, "The Apprentice." He was a businessman, not a TV star, so that within of itself caused a bit of concern. In addition he had to deal with the negative critics or tormentors. He had to endure comments such as, "Most new TV shows fail," "Reality TV is on it's way out," among other negative comments.

Trumps says that it was hard dealing with the pressure, but he chose to concentrate on the positive. So instead of focusing on "what if the show failed?" he chose to focus on "what if it's a hit?" He chose not to focus on the fact that critics were saying that "Reality TV is on its way out." He chose to focus on the fact that "Reality TV is in now."

Contrapreneurs like Trump understand that success is a process, and when they encounter trouble, they keep on pressing, and you have to learn to do the same.

This may be somewhat challenging, but always remember that perception is greater than reality. In many cases, perception is reality. It's all about how you perceive a situation. Is the glass half empty or is it half full? Is your business about to go under, or is your business poised for a miraculous turnaround? Did someone just take advantage of you, or did they teach you an important lesson for the future? It's all about staying positive and keeping the proper perspective.

My tendency is to be a relatively positive person, but it takes a lot of practice and repetition. I wasn't born with a positive attitude, I had to develop it. It takes effort.

Here are five quick tips that have helped me to keep it positive. I'm 100 percent sure that there's something here for you, too.

## TIP #1 – BUILD AN ARK

In the Bible, the book of Exodus records the history of the nation of Israel and their escape from Egyptian bondage. The book begins by speaking of the oppression that Israel faced by the Egyptian Pharaoh. The Israelites had no freedom and no rights. They were told what to do and had the harsh task of making brick without straw.

In the book, God sent a deliverer by the name of Moses to free Israel. As the story goes, Moses was successful in freeing Israel, and after crossing the Red Sea, God began to give Moses instructions, or keys for success. Moses was also given a number of tasks, including that of building a tabernacle and he was also instructed to build an ark.

This ark was not like Noah's ark, but rather a treasure chest, or a keepsake box, only on a grander scale. God then told Moses to put into the box the testimony that He gave to them. He later instructed them to add a few other items such as the 10 Commandments and Aaron's rod that budded – all reminders of where they had come from and how they made it out.

I'll get back to the ark in a second. Isn't it strange how we have a tendency to remember negative things more easily than the positive? Isn't it funny that we can go through a situation, feel like it is so horrible that we'll never make it out and wonder if we'll even survive? We go through all of the worry only to discover that the worry doesn't change a thing. Then we come through the situation just fine. We are elated and thankful, but when we find ourselves going go through another situation a few months later, we rarely remember the last situation we successfully came out of.

We have a tendency to forget the good, because we're so busy experiencing the bad. People who don't understand this natural human tendency will tend to be on the negative side. God understood this about human nature, so He instructed Moses to build an ark that would serve as a reminder of what they had accomplished. He wanted them to remember how many times they'd "made it through." He also wanted them to be reminded of their potential power.

Like Moses, I found myself needing a serious ark after the Magic Show. Remember that? I'll never forget the Magic Show!

After the Magic Show, I came back to Austin sad and depressed, wondering how I was going to pay the money back that had been borrowed, not to mention how my mortgage would be paid and don't forget living expenses. How was I going to eat? I began to envy my older brother who had graduated from college two years earlier. He moved back home to San Antonio to live with my parents. He was working in corporate America and had no real bills to pay.

Ironically, he worked at the same rental car company that I previously interned with. I actually got him hired. Although, it was clear that happiness would not be found living with my parents, working a "good job," deep down that was my desire.

As a result of my dilemma, I decided to go into real estate full-time, but there was a small problem. Okay, a BIG problem. At that time, my transportation was a 10 year-old Mazda B2600 that had to be kick-started every morning.

I had no reliable transportation. I couldn't take clients around looking at houses in an old jalopy truck like mine. Not to mention it was only a two-seater. I was really worried and had no idea what I would do.

One day I decided to go look for a car, just to see what was available. Maybe I can get a loan, I thought. Sure, it would put me further in debt, but it was my only hope.

While at a local dealer, I looked at a few cars, and picked out a beautiful maroon Nissan Maxima. My dream car had been a

Maxima since seeing the movie "Menace to Society" my junior year in high school. The salesman told me the price would run somewhere in the neighborhood of $18,000, which, of course, I couldn't afford. Then, he told me I'd need a $3,000 down payment. Ouch!

I walked away like a child that had just dropped his snow cone in the dirt. In my mind, the dream was dead. From all indications, I was headed back to corporate America. Then, on a whim, I thought, "Let me call Dad. Maybe he can help with the down payment."

If you knew my Dad, then you knew this was not a phone call that I was eager to make, but I was so desperate that I dialed the number and held my breath.

"Uh, Dad," I paused. "I'm at the Nissan dealership, because I've got to get a new car. The one I'm driving is breaking down on me, and I wanted to see if you might be able to help."

"How much is the darn car?" That's the PG version of what he really said.

"The down payment is $3,000," I responded. Dad wasn't big on small talk.

"That's not what I asked," he said. "How much is the darn car?"

I hesitated and took a deep breath. "$18,000." I figured that would be the end of the call, but then Dad said eight words that proceeded to shock me.

"It'll be in your account in 30 minutes."

Dad always taught me to stay out of debt. "Never owe anyone," he'd say. This same guy had just deposited 18 G's into my account and I was able to buy the car cash! Cash!

Now, for some of you, maybe that's nothing, but for someone who didn't grow up with much, that was huge!

My parents were very conservative. We always had a roof over our heads and food to eat, but I was the kid who wore hand-me-downs from my brother, so you can imagine that my Dad's generosity was not only surprising but also overwhelming. I had no idea my parents were in a position to flat out give me $18,000 cash. This was yet another miracle!

Imagine my posture when getting off the phone and telling the car salesman to skip the down payment. "I'm paying with cash." I was exhibiting a whole new confidence.

So what's the point? Prior to me buying the car, I felt desperate and hopeless. I didn't know what I was going to do, yet in a matter of minutes, my feeling was that I could accomplish anything. Following God's counsel to Moses I built my own ark! Mine was not as grand as the one in the Bible of course, but it helped to serve a similar purpose.

I wanted to be reminded of my potential, so I went to a local store and bought the biggest jewelry box available. It has in it various trinkets to serve as reminders of what I'd been through.

Some of the items in my ark included the HUD statement from my first real estate property, bought at age 21, a copy of my first logo with GUGOGS, a vendor badge from the first Houston Black Expo, and the deed for my Maxima miracle.

During stressful times that challenge my emotional climate, I go to my ark and take a long look at those forget-me-nots. I'm immediately reminded of my past accomplishments, and they give me the motivation to press on.

Now, don't get hung up on the jewelry box. An ark doesn't have to be a jewelry box, or even a box at all. It can simply be a place that you keep reminders of previous successes. It should include items that have the ability to take you back to your past, invoke your emotions, and help you keep your emotional climate on a positive note.

What about you? What's in your home or office to remind you of your successes?

## TIP #2: GET IN SHAPE...STAY IN SHAPE

Fitness advice in a business book? Absolutely. If you allow your mental and physical health to suffer, you won't be around long enough to enjoy the "fruits" of your business and contrapreneurial labor.

If you're going to have a successful business, it is important that you remain fit, both physically and mentally. Remaining fit will go a long way in keeping you positive and keeping your energy and excitement levels high. Running a business takes a great deal of time, right? That's why living a healthy lifestyle, complete with regular exercise, is essential. What good does it do for you to amass wealth if you aren't here to enjoy it?

First, you need to establish an exercise routine. This is of the utmost importance. I once heard a physician pose a poignant question. "Have you ever seen stagnant water?"

He went on to explain that in stagnant water you have all types of bacteria, fungus, and other unhealthy things that begin to grow and thrive. However, if you put a fountain in the water, and the water is continuously stirred, the bacteria and fungus can't grow as readily, and it won't attract as many bugs. Our bodies are two-thirds water. If we're stagnant, watching TV all day or sitting in front of a computer all day at work, the water in our bodies will not be stirred, which creates an environment for bacteria and disease to grow. In order to prevent this, we must get regular physical activity. In other words, movement keeps our systems in check.

> Add more fruits, vegetables and whole grains to your diet and watch your "engine" rev up like a finely tuned machine.

The next thing we have to do is get our recommended doses of vitamins. Did you know that in 1940 one serving of an orange gave you the necessary daily supply of Vitamin C?

Today, you'd have to eat as many as ten oranges to get an

equal amount of Vitamin C. The primary reason for this is quite simple.

Over the years, our farmlands and soil have been tremendously overworked, and they have been depleted and robbed of vital minerals and nutrients necessary to produce crops as nutritional as they were in 1940. In essence, you may be eating what would be called "healthy foods," but they are not as healthy as they should be. Taking a good multivitamin can help compensate for this lack of nutritional value in our food.

The final piece of the health puzzle is proper nutrition. Everyone's body is different. No two bodies are going to need the same exercise, vitamins or nutrition. Think of your body as its own individual car. In order to function properly, it needs fuel. If you put cheap, low quality fuel into your car's tank, it will not function at optimal capacity. The same is true for our bodies. Stay away from cheap fast food, sweets, and other foods that are notorious for compromising our body's many systems. Add more fruits, vegetables, and whole grains to your diet, and watch your "engine" rev up like a finely tuned machine!

## TIP #3: USE YOUR WORDS WISELY

Words help to shape and frame our emotional climate. They have the power to lodge in our subconscious and appear at an opportune time to torment us. That's why you have to speak positive words into the atmosphere and into your own heart.

Muhammad Ali was a master at speaking power into being. You'd see him in interviews, and he'd say things like, "I'm the greatest, and no one can beat me." He'd then go on to talk about his opponents, how they were no competition, and how badly he'd beat them. Those were important words, as they helped to energize and charge him up.

In addition to charging him up, his words energized everyone around him, but here's what is even more amazing about Ali's words. Upon hearing him on the radio or seeing him on television, his opponents would start to second-guess themselves. Did Ali's words make him the best boxer of his time? No. He had to back up those words with a strong work ethic. However, the one thing Muhammad Ali did better than anyone else was show us that who we become starts with the words we use to describe ourselves. He was the first to say he was "The Greatest," but he wasn't the last.

## TIP #4: WRITE YOURSELF A LETTER

I received my first Franklin Covey binder upon starting in the real estate business full time in 2000. One of the sections within the binder is the daily planner. This area is where you list all of the daily activities that you need to accomplish in a particular day. All of the new real estate agents were given these planners along with extensive training.

During the training, one of the things they told us about the daily planner section was to write our activities for "that" day the "day before" while we were still thinking clearly. They strongly urged us not to make these entries while we were still at the office, or on the way to the office because doing so would affect our ability to truly get things done. We were taught to plan our day in advance when we were relaxed. I encourage you to write yourself a letter outlining what you expect to happen in your business. Include as much detail as possible, and make sure you plan the positive and the negative. This will help to serve as a point of reference when you begin to experience hardship within your business.

For instance, in January of 2003, I wrote a letter regarding the Houston Black Expo. The letter included how excited I was about the opportunity, how pleased I was with the web design, and how I had acquired my seed money. This letter would serve as that "positive" reminder when things got rough, as I knew they probably would. It was important for me to have an archive, if you will, of those assets mentioned in an earlier section. I knew that there would come a day when I would need a big shot from Dr. Feelgood. This letter was going to be my Dr. Feelgood. It was going to be the encouragement needed to stay the course and make my dreams a reality. So, as you can see, this letter was of supreme importance.

Once I'd gotten all of the positive things written down, I also acknowledged that most businesses fail within the first year, and that no profits should be anticipated for at least five years. Even though I wrote all those things, deep down, I did not expect things to be quite that bad. However, after the Expo in 2004, that was my reality: I found myself $80,000 in the hole, no salary, a six-month old baby girl at home and no foreseeable income. At the time, this letter was all I had. I was what some people would call being "down on your luck."

A preacher once said that the man with no shoes feels sorry for himself until he sees the man with no feet. In order to remain positive, you have to remain positive. You have to do whatever it takes to keep your head up. No matter what adversity arises, you can overcome it.

So, fire up the computer and get that letter started. You'll be glad you did!

## TIP #5: EXPECT THE BEST, PREPARE FOR THE WORST

Remember my excitement when I conceived the Black Expo? I knew it had tremendous potential. I envisioned myself with lots of money, being recognized within the community, and winning awards for my efforts. I remember putting together my business plan and budget estimates and then shopping them around to potential investors. Man, I couldn't be stopped, and I was ready for the world!

I had the money, business cards, folders and other marketing materials, but for some reason, the fish weren't biting. I recall re-reading the book, Permission Marketing to hone my marketing materials and sales pitch in order to raise sponsor dollars. I spent months sending proposals and leaving messages, all with no luck. I began to get frustrated, wondering if I'd maybe eaten some bad pasta that was now causing me to hallucinate and think that I could pull this thing off.

The debt was mounting, my angel investor backed out on me, and I didn't know what I'd do to survive. Even when $80,000 of debt was staring me in the face, I still saw so much potential, so it was frustrating not having the resources to do what was needed. It was hard to stay positive, but I knew that there had to be a way to succeed.

I once heard a speaker say, "You get what you expect." I was expecting great things to happen, but they weren't happening, at least not yet.

Soon, though, it was time to put up or shut up. I already knew that most businesses don't see any profit in their first year, so I just decided to bite the bullet and forge ahead. The primary goal was to get that "first" Expo done, so I put on the army boots and went to battle. When the first event was done, I breathed a sigh of relief. I celebrated the birth of the first Houston Black Expo. And while that first event left me in the red, the journey was far from complete. There was only a month's break before I'd have to start working on Year Two's Expo.

Regular sacrifices had to be made in order to make sure my business survived. My family put off our plans for the new home, choosing instead to hang out in our little 30-year-old home, dealing with all of the issues that come along with many 30-year-old houses.

To make ends meet, I had to substitute teach on the side while continuing with real estate. Needless to say, it was a hard 11 months leading up to our second annual Houston Black Expo, but we made it! We doubled our attendance, increased our sponsorships, and had a great time. Even so, in the end, we only made enough to cover the expenses for that particular Expo…and we were still $80,000 in the hole!

Nonetheless, things were looking up, and I needed to look on the bright side of things. Now the business had a clear identity and brand awareness. The community began to recognize our organization. Sponsors started soliciting us rather than us banging down their doors. It was obvious that there was still a lot of life in the business. My only question was, "Am I ever going to get out of debt?"

To add insult to injury, we now had the pain and frustration of dodging lawsuits, going to court, and spending money we didn't have on attorneys. I kept reminding myself: this is a marathon, not a sprint. Just keep running.

I kept the faith and continued to keep my eyes on the prize.

They say genius hits you when you least expect it, and I couldn't agree more. One day we came up with a brilliant idea: the Houston Black Expo "Lunch & Learn," a monthly seminar that would help develop small businesses. We also put together the HBE "Veteran Vendor" special and offered a discount program for returning vendors. This created another revenue stream during that 11-month waiting period that helped us keep the lights on and hope alive. When your business is struggling, instead of getting down on yourself, do as we did: bring your team together and do a "brainstorming" session. Think of all the ways you could possibly increase your business or reduce your costs. The goal is to get creative!

Money's probably not going to just fall from the sky. At least it didn't in Houston! Knowing that the health of my business rested squarely on my shoulders, I didn't have a whole lot of time to feel sorry for myself. I needed to be in the game at full tilt. I needed to act like I was getting ready for the big game — every single day! I needed to lace up my sneakers, get hydrated, and settle in for a marathon, not a sprint. The road got a little rocky and that's why I kept saying, "Keep running. You'll get there, but you gotta keep running."

So that's what I did.

The year 2006 was tough but it was also what I call our "silver lining" year. In 2006, we realized our first profit. And guess what? I got my first check!

In 2007, it got even better when I got my second check, which was more than three times what had been issued in 2006.

While we still have a lot of growth potential, I know we're on our way. Writing this, I'm reminded of that saying, "The race is not given to the swift or the strong but to the one that endures."

Keep running, contrapreneurs. You'll get there.

# ELEVEN

# Confidence is the Key

---

*"Contrapreneurship has really inspired me and changed the direction that I am taking with my business. This book is a powerful roadmap to success in business."*

**—Darryl White, Owner, Done Right Home Repair & Services**

"I'm a baaaaaaaaaaaad man!"

Those are the words that repeatedly came out of Muhammad Ali's mouth during the peak of his boxing career. If Ali lacked anything, it wasn't confidence. He wasn't afraid to tell opponents what he'd do to them. He wasn't afraid to tell you why he was "the greatest." Whether or not you agree with Ali's assessment of himself is irrelevant. He built an international persona based on his confidence. That, my friends, is a powerful tool.

Why is your business the greatest? Why are you the greatest at what you do? Do you have the skills but lack the confidence? Then listen up.

Confidence is the key to success in business and life in general. You have to be confident in who you are. You must recognize that you were created in the image of God. He has placed a hidden treasure within you, and it is your job to search and dig for that treasure. You can't look for other people to define who you are. You have to know and come to that for yourself.

## LIKE MIKE...OR LIKE YOU?

One of the first things that you learn in business is the concept of supply and demand. The relationship between these two components determines the value of a particular commodity. The greater the supply, the lower the demand, and the less a certain commodity is valued. This relationship is the driving force behind a free market. When one entity has exclusive control over a commodity, it is called a monopoly. Although it may be profitable, it is strictly prohibited.

I'm not trying to give you a crash course in economics, but I do want to remind you that you're a monopoly. You are the commodity. There has never been, and there will never be another you, thus your value is limitless. Until you fully understand this fundamental concept, others will try to put a value on you and define who you are. Further, the more you try to be like everyone else or conform to what others want you to be, the less valuable you become in the marketplace and ultimately within yourself. Value is always found in your individual uniqueness.

When I created the Houston Black Expo I was seeking to become more of who I already was, but I was also seeking to bring more value, more uniqueness to the marketplace.

> Contrapreneurs go against the grain, they're not like everyone else.

Part of my job with the Houston Black Expo is to secure exhibitors, so I travel regularly to trade shows to seek out new customers. Once, I attended an event where on the first aisle, there was a purse in the style that my wife likes, so I decided to buy it for her. It was the perfect style and the price was right, but they didn't take credit cards, so I had to go to an ATM machine for cash.

Before going to the ATM, I walked a few more aisles, and saw about three other vendors with the same purse. At that point, the value of the first purse decreased. I was ready to buy when my thought was that there would not be another deal that great. Yet, when finding the same purse in three different places, I went back to each and negotiated a lower price. My point is this: if you can get the same thing in other places, the value that you ascribe to a particular item decreases. The lesson for us all is: don't try to be like everyone else, for your value is in being you.

Russell Simmons is arguably the most important businessman in rap music history and co-founder of Def Jam Records, and he lives by this principle. Simmons was instrumental in developing rap music into the big business that it is today, and at one point built his communication company to be the largest black-owned enterprise in the industry. He later sold Def Jam for a reported $100 million and is still one of the recognizable figures in the industry.

In his book, Do you, he notes that of all the laws of success that he believes in and strives to live by, the law of 'Do You' is the most important.

Simmons states, "I always follow the Law of Do You, which stresses staying true to who you are and what you like instead of following trends."

Simmons is a great example of a contrapreneur.

Contrapreneurs go against the grain. They're not like everyone else. They understand that their value is in their uniqueness. We live in a society that tries to press people to conform to a particular way of being. Think about it. Gatorade made millions and millions of dollars in the '90s, with the campaign "Like Mike." Everyone wanted to be like Michael Jordan, but there was only one Mike. What would have happened if Phoenix Suns guard and two-time NBA MVP Steve Nash had gotten discouraged because he couldn't dunk from the free throw line like Jordan? Or if Shaquille O'Neal tried to shoot free throws like Indiana Pacers great, Reggie Miller? Aside from the Miami Heat being thrilled about the Big Aristotle's charity line percentages, Shaq wouldn't be Shaq, would he?

My point is that when an individual recognizes his or her own unique gift and talents, they create their own niche, and their value is limitless.

# TWELVE

# Contrast Hunting with Fishing

---

*"As the title sponsor of the Houston Black Expo, since its inception, I have had the chance to work closely with Jerome for the past fours years. It has been a pleasure and a blessing to see him move his God given vision into a reality. Professionally speaking, it has been a pleasure working with him and watching him grow."*

**—James E. Harris, Director, Supplier Diversity, H-E-B**

There are a number of key elements that are necessary to build a successful business. Of all the ingredients necessary for business success, one of the most important elements is having a hungry market that is willing to buy your product or service.

So how are you going to reach these people? How will they

know that you exist? When you get their attention, what will you say? Will you do mail-outs? Will you buy TV commercials or radio time? These are all questions that must be answered in order to build your customer base. You must think like a contrapreneur, not like the average business owner.

## TOO MUCH INFORMATION...OR SMART MARKETING?

Traditional marketing and advertising are not as effective as they once were. Back in the early to mid 1900's, technology wasn't as advanced as it is today. The pace was much slower 100 years ago, and 20 years ago, the choices for advertising were quite limited. You only had two to three television stations to choose from, and less than a dozen radio stations. There was no Internet, no cell phones, and no billboards off the freeway. The way people thought about marketing and advertising was quite different. If you had a salesman knock on your door, you would have been more likely to talk to the salesman.

Today we are inundated with technological advances. We are constantly bombarded with thousands of advertisements and unsolicited requests daily. You have billboards, TV ads, Internet ads, pop-ups, and even cell phone advertisements. I was even in the restroom at my gym one day and noticed ads in front of the urinals. There are now TVs at the gas pumps!

Seth Godin, in his book Permission Marketing, refers to this advertising as "interruption marketing." That's why it's now routinely confronted with hostility and disdain.

Godin defines advertising as the science of creating and placing media that interrupts the consumer in an attempt to get him or her to take action. Traditional advertising used to be more effective. However, with the typical consumer being interrupted by these messages on average 3,000 times daily, more and more of these messages are being viewed as un-welcomed distractions.

I couldn't agree more. When I'm at the urinal, I don't really need to see an ad staring me in the face. I'm there to do my business and leave. When I'm on hold with my bank, do I really need to hear about the latest and greatest innovation in cellular technology? When I'm shopping for groceries, is it really necessary to put an ad on my shopping cart? Apparently, advertisers believe that they must blanket every open space with their message. What they don't realize is that consumers can become so inundated with advertising messages that they lose their impact and effectiveness. Why? Because the message is more of a distraction.

Here's an example that I know a lot of you can identify with.

Let's say it's the day before Thanksgiving, and the store is jam packed. Your boss lets you off from work at noon. You're trying to get all of the necessary items to make the holiday meal. You're running late, but you need to go pick up your in-laws from the airport, and get your kids from daycare, which, by the way, will be closing early at 2:30 p.m. on that day. While at the store, you're solicited by the Salvation Army, the Christmas tree vendor in the parking lot, and the cute little Girl Scout troupe that's selling holiday cookies. To make matters worse, you've also got a migraine that won't stop!

Now, what are you most likely to do? Are you going to give the Salvation Army guy any change? Are you going to buy a Christmas tree? As cute as they are, are the little girls going to persuade you to pony up seven bucks for a box of cookies? Probably not.

Why? Because their message is a pest! It really doesn't matter how great your product or service is, because you, the advertiser, are an unwanted distraction —in that particular moment. Consumers throw away your direct mail pieces, hang up on the cold calls, and flip to one of the other 500 or so channels at the commercial breaks during their favorite television show. Knocking your consumers over the head with advertising is what I call hunting for business, and no one wants to be hunted.

Now, let's take the flip side of that story, and let's say that you're shopping at 7:30 at night when the store is relatively quiet. You're listening to the music, and a song you like is playing. You get your shopping done with little or no fanfare. There's no Salvation Army person and no Christmas tree vendor hounding you, but those little girls are just about to wrap up and head home when one of them approaches you as you head out the door. "Would you like to buy a box of cookies?"

What are you likely to do? Do they have a better chance of landing a sale now that you don't have a migraine and you're not being bombarded by a thousand advertising messages? Of course! Heck, you might even buy two boxes, right?

Guess what? Now you know what your customers go through

every day. Armed with this knowledge, you can now attempt to position your message at the right time and in the right format. Only then will you have a good shot at earning their business.

## HUNTING VS. FISHING

If you're going to be successful in attracting new customers and building your business, you have to learn the difference between fishing and hunting. Both may help to close sales and put food on the table, however, fishing is a more effective way to make a living. Unlike hunting, fishing is less labor intensive, and it isn't met with hostility. Before discussing fishing, let's look at what happens when a business owner operates like a hunter so that you can see what not to do.

## WHAT'S WRONG WITH HUNTING?

There are several definitions for the word "hunt." I'm going to focus on one definition, which entails pursuing with force and hostility in order to capture. When you think about the concept of pursuit, you think about a predator and its prey. The natural instinct of the prey when it is being hunted or pursued with hostility is to run, avoid contact, and create distance. That's the consumer or potential client.

Hunters know that the natural inclination of the prey is to run when being hunted. As a result, the hunter has to wear camouflage in an attempt to disguise his presence and to blend into the background so that he doesn't stand out. He must duck and hide in the bushes, sometimes for hours at a time, so that he will not be seen. A hunter has to keep his voice down and alter his speech so as not to alert the prey. In watching nature shows,

> [Contrapreneurial businessmen and women] have the freedom to be who they are and also recognize that the more distinct they are, and the more they separate themselves from the rest, the more attractive they become.

I've seen hunters actually mimic the sound of the desired prey. The hunter waits for the opportune time and, when that time comes, he subdues his unsuspecting prey with force. Pow!

While hunters eventually achieve their goal of making a kill, it is always at the expense of the unsuspecting prey. Hunters have to be deceitful and very careful about hiding their true identity.

They have to change their clothing and change the way they sound so that they aren't detected. In other words, they try to appear to be something that they are not. Although hunting may result in a kill, it's an outdated and archaic way to put food on the table. It is a method in which the hunter is simply consumed with himself and his desire to survive. He is selfish, and no one likes a selfish individual.

This is the same way that many businessmen and women operate today. They change their clothes and put on their finest suits. They change the way they talk to try to sound more professional. They disguise their true identities and motives until the unsuspecting customer is at his or her most vulnerable point and then the hunter pounces on them. The hunter has hidden in the bushes—cold calling random people — or knocking on doors, hoping for the opportunity to get a clean shot, or that coveted appointment. They are not concerned about the customer's needs; they are simply concerned about making the sale so that they can survive. Sometimes it may work, but remember, it always comes at the expense of the unsuspecting customer.

## WHY FISHING IS A BETTER OPTION

Fishing is a vastly superior method of making the catch. I define fishing as presenting something desirable in order to attract something desirable.

When you hunt, the instinctive reaction of the catch is to flee or to run, as opposed to fishing, where the natural instinct is to draw closer. A fisherman is free to wear whatever he chooses. In fact, the brighter the color, the better. The more he stands out from the crowd or background, the more attractive he becomes. That's why fisherman put on their bright orange life preservers. They cast their lines with the right bait, and the fish are drawn to the bait.

As a kid growing up in Lake Providence, Louisiana, I had the opportunity to go fishing on several occasions. Most of the adults I knew either fished regularly or knew a lot about fishing. I knew people who would set up two or three poles with bait or a net, go run errands, and then come back hours later and find the catch for the day.

Unlike hunters, fishermen don't have to work nearly as hard in order to make a catch. It's much easier. Even when the fisherman was not there, the fish were still attracted and being drawn into his net.

The same principles hold true for contrapreneurial businessmen and women who know how to fish. They are attractive. They know what the fish or customer wants. They have the freedom to be who they are and also recognize that the more distinct they are, and the more they separate themselves from the rest, the more attractive they become. They are not deceptive, and as a result, fish willingly draw nearer to them. They don't have to work for hours sitting in the bushes cold calling or knocking down doors; rather, they can go to the gym to work out or even on vacation and know that fish are still being drawn to their bait. You see, fishing is a far more effective way to make a sale. All successful fishermen must possess one key skill, so listen up.

## HIGH FISH IQ

A good fisherman understands fish. He has taken the time to study and observe their behavior. He knows their likes and dislikes. A fisherman knows when fish like to eat and when they don't. He knows what dangers or concerns they have within their natural environment. He studies where they like to hang out and gather, and knows where they typically live. He understands what makes a fish tick, if you will.

Every year in Louisiana around March and April, Dad would wake me up at the crack of dawn, at four or five o'clock in the morning before the sun came up. What did Dad want? To go fishing, of course. We'd load up his old pickup truck and drive into town to go fishing. He'd always bring a couple of bologna sandwiches and stop by the corner store to pick us up a couple honey buns. In the little town that we lived in, they had huge levies that we'd drive up on, and then we would go down to the bank to do our fishing.

When we'd get out on the lake my dad would instruct me on how to put the bait on the hook and cast my line. He taught me to always cast my line near old tree stumps or bushes. As a kid, I really wasn't that concerned about the fish. I was trying to have fun, so I'd throw my line all over the place, which meant that I typically didn't come home with any fish, or nowhere near as many as my Dad. Why? Dad had a higher fish IQ than I did. He understood fish.

Dad knew that fish liked cool water, so even though it wasn't convenient for me to wake up at four o'clock in the morning, it was the perfect time to fish before the hot sun came out. He also knew that fish had an instinctive need to spawn every March and April, which meant that they would come closer to the banks.

Dad was an experienced fisherman who knew that fish like to hide from potential predators near stumps and in the brush. He also knew that algae would develop on old tree stumps, which the small minnows ate, and minnows were a favorite meal of the fish.

Thus, if you had a tree stump, your chances of making a catch increased. Of all the things that Dad taught me about fishing, the last was the most important and yet the simplest. He told me that fish only eat when they're hungry. Dad's vast knowledge of fish enabled him to catch more fish than anyone. The smart contrapreneur, like Dad, studies the customers, knows the market, and as a result, is able to draw fish all day long.

Fish only eat when they're hungry? What a concept!

Many times, entrepreneurs forget this simple yet profound

little fact. They create a product or service that they think is wonderful. They never stop to think about whether or not the consumer has an appetite for their product or service. Then, when they cast their lines but catch no fish, they become frustrated, wondering why they can't catch any fish!

Donald Trump states that if you are going to be success in any business you have to know who you are talking to and where he or she is coming from. In his book Trump 101 he warns readers, not to be so involved in trying to get what they want that they don't think of anyone but themselves. He also states that you can't be so overcome with the brilliance of your idea that you ignore other people's needs and objectives, because if you do it will prohibit you from successfully connecting with your customer.

I challenge you: before you begin to market and advertise your business, stop and think. Think about your fish; think about what they need, and what they want. Remember that customers like to be courted, but they don't like to be preyed upon. Give the fish what they like to eat — at the time that they like to eat — and you'll catch fish all day, everyday!

# THIRTEEN

# Congratulate Yourself!

*"At last an easy to read book for new & aspiring business owners struggling with getting started. Contrapreneurship has inspired me to stop talking about starting my business & to do it."*

**—Onaje Barnes, Real Estate Investor**

You did it! You took a big step toward creating a powerful business empire. You bought this book, and you finished it! Congratulations!

Let me remind you of your power. I'm going to be your verbal "ark."

Contrapreneurs are unique individuals. They're not like everyone else. They have a unique vision. They see what others can not see. Therefore, you cannot look to others to affirm or disaffirm your vision. No one has the ability to see your vision the way you do, because it's YOUR vision!

Contrapreneurs are trendsetters. We are trailblazers, and we are forerunners. In short, we are leaders. The status quo has never worked for us, and it never will. When others are going right, we're confident enough to stay with our decision to go left. Even though going left may mean that we have to walk alone sometimes, contrapreneurs will continue to make big strides, knowing that others will soon follow.

I'll leave you with one quick story that I believe sums up this journey we're on together.

Remember the Encyclopedia salesmen? When I was younger, about once a year, we'd get that knock on the door. You know the knock I'm talking about. The Encyclopedia Guy. He'd wear that slick polyester or double knit suit, a pair of cheap shoes and a mega watt smile.

Every house in my neighborhood had a set of Encyclopedias. We sure did. If you had a question about anything from your body to reptiles to the solar system, where was the first place you'd look? The Encyclopedia! If I had a book report to write,

I went to the Encyclopedia.

They'd try to sell us on the latest edition. Even though we already had the previous edition, which took up two whole rows on our bookshelf, my parents would always buy a new set to make sure that we had the latest information.

Imagine if the good folks behind the Encyclopedia Britannica, had been a bit more forward-thinking. What if they'd seen the Internet coming? What if in the mid to early nineties they had registered, and properly marketed Encyclopedia.com?

It would have been a natural progression for the millions of people across the world to throw away those old obsolete, big and bulky, Encyclopedias, and to log on to Encyclopedia.com. If they had made the proper adjustment, would there even be a Google or Yahoo? Encyclopedia.com arguably would have been the most visited site on the web, hands down.

Encyclopedia Britannica, though still profitable, could have been a monster force in the world of information. Yet, because they were reactive instead of proactive, they didn't reach their full business potential.

Today, right now, you're sitting on an idea. Maybe your

business needs to go to the next level, but for some reason you're not taking that next step. You're like the Encyclopedia people. Waiting for inspiration while the rest of the world is passing you by. Guess what? You can no longer afford to react to the world.

Contrapreneurs like you and I are paving the way for new technology, new innovations and new inventions. There are no limits, and quite honestly, there are no more excuses.

So, the real question for you today is this, "How high do you want to soar?"

I've given you the tools to see business differently and most importantly, to DO business differently.

The ball, as we say, is now in your court.

Always remember, success in not a matter of chance, but a matter of choice! It's up to you.